THE TELEVISION WRITER'S HANDBOOK

What to Write, How to Write It, Where to Sell It

CONSTANCE NASH
and
VIRGINIA OAKEY

BARNES & NOBLE BOOKS

A DIVISION OF HARPER & ROW, PUBLISHERS

New York, Hagerstown, San Francisco, London

Grateful acknowledgment is made for permission to reprint the following materials:

Excerpt from teleplay "Kingdom in the Dust" reprinted by permission of Isabelle Ziegler.

Excerpts from teleplay "The Rookies"—"Blue Christmas" reprinted by permission of Aaron Spelling.

Excerpt from teleplay "You're Not Getting Better, Just Older" from *Phyllis.* © MCMLXXVI MTM Enterprises. All rights reserved.

Designed by Eve Callahan

FIRST EDITION

PN
1992.7
. N3

LIBRARY OF CONGRESS CATALOG CARD NUMBER: 77–77788

ISBN: 0–06–013161–6

ISBN: 0–06–463455–8 (PBK)

83 84 85 86   10 9 8 7 6

Contents

Acknowledgments

—Our warmest thanks to Eric Weissmann, our legal mentor, whose professional advice and encouragement have been of immeasurable value to us.

—Our gratitude to all of our interviewees who responded so graciously and generously to all of our questions asked on your behalf: Blanche Hanalis, Aaron Spelling, Tony Ford, and Stuart Christenfeld.

—Our particular thanks to Aaron Spelling for his permission to use many excerpts from his teleplay *Blue Christmas* from *The Rookies* series; to MTM Enterprises, Inc.; to David Lloyd for permission to use excerpts from the teleplay *You're Not Getting Better, Just Older* from the *Phyllis* series; and to Isabelle Ziegler for permission to use excerpts from her treatment for the teleplay *Kingdom in the Dust.*

—Our appreciation for valuable assistance received from Louis Rudolph, ABC executive, John Schallert, agent; Ed Friendly, producer; Michael H. Franklin, executive director of the Writers Guild of America, West, Inc.; The American Film Institute Library, and the Writers Guild of America, West, Inc.

The Essential Elements

Teleplays, like all other art forms, require certain basic components that are used as building materials to create something which has depth, breadth, and substance.

First of these teleplay components is the *concept,* whether it emerges from a fantasized character or situation, from an experience, or from a philosophical persuasion. Second is the *plot,* the framework within which you will expand your fantasy or vision. But the framework, strong as it may be, cannot stand alone. It must be filled in, given both body and dynamism. This is achieved through your skillful use of *characterization* and *dialog.* A knowledge of how to write and use *narrative* is essential to a fully realized script. These components—concept, plot, characterization, dialog, and narrative —are mandatory to the fulfillment of your dramatic purpose, and everything depends upon the way you use them.

HOW TO PLAN YOUR TELEPLAY: CONCEPT AND PLOT

Before you come to grips with your plot, you should understand the possibilities and limitations of television. First, it is a more intimate stage than the big screen. The movie theater has become the viewer's living room. The wide screen has narrowed to a console or a 9-inch battery set. The viewer is practically eyeball to eyeball with the screen images, so for him or her the experience is much more intimate than in the theater. When your teleplay is screened it will be seen by millions of persons, it is to be hoped. Yet television is a medium aimed at a few persons gathered cozily around a set in the home. Second, greater discipline is needed for teleplay writing than for movie writing. Time is a product for sale on television, so all scripts must be tailored to specific time slots—30, 60, 90, 120 minutes (see chapter 3). Your scripts must be tightly constructed so that they do not run over or fall short. However, these limits have a certain flexibility since cuts can always be made during the final editing. You do not have the latitude, in terms of script lengths, that filmwriters have, though. Right now, don't overly concern yourself with the time requirements except for one thing: if you decide to write a 30-minute script, don't try to include material with enough scope for a novel; a 120-minute script, however, may cover as much territory as a novel or movie. (*The Autobiography of Miss Jane Pittman,* a teleplay by Tracy Keenan Wynn, covers the entire life of a very old woman from her early childhood.)

Television has been with us for more than a quarter of a century. If you are twenty-five or younger, you have been a viewer ever since you could crawl over and turn the knob. If you are older, you still have had twenty-five years of television viewing. Whichever age group you fall into, you have spent thousands of hours watching television. By now you know which shows or types of shows attract you, and these probably are the ones for which you should try to write. However, if you are tuned in especially to episodic dramas but have a real talent for comedy, you might best serve that talent by writing comedy. We don't mean that you should not try dramatic scripts, but in the beginning it is wise to flow with your first talent. When you have mastered comedy, then you can branch out. The possibilities for diverse writing in television are limitless.

Now let's get back to you, sitting at your desk, ready to begin planning your teleplay. Decide whether your concept will be best developed through emphasis on (1) character, (2) theme, or (3) situation. Most teleplays will contain all three, but your initial concept will dictate which one the stress will be on.

The Autobiography of Miss Jane Pittman is a prime example of a teleplay in which the emphasis is on the main character or protagonist. *QB VII*, the *theme* of which is one man's relentless search for truth against incredible opposition, is an example of a thematic script, despite its very strong characterizations. Shows that are more concerned with the *situation* and ensuing action include all the police action shows such as *Streets of San Francisco* and *Police Woman*. The continuing characters are well established, but the plots are focused on the action, not the actors.

Whichever you choose, hold tightly to your original idea so that your script will maintain balance and integrity of purpose. Don't change direction midway; your plot will become muddled and diffused, and your teleplay will fall apart.

CONFLICT AND CRISES

Conflict is the moving force of drama. Stories must be told through the presentation of a problem or problems that your characters meet head on and have to overcome or be overcome by. Develop the plot through these problems. They can have a wide range—from a child's need to find a lost dog to a man's need to revenge the murder-rape of his daughter. They do not have to be heart-shattering but they must touch the nerve ends of the viewers. It must be made clear why or how they occur and how they are resolved. The most traumatic moments for your characters are the crises (or plot points) around which your teleplay will be constructed. All action builds up to these crises and each indicates a turning point in the plot, whether it is severe or subtle.

CLIMAX

Before you write a word on paper, know what the climax will be —the moment at which all the problems are resolved. Everything leads to this moment; it is your destination, and if you lose sight of it the ending may not be as sharp and forceful as it should be. Perhaps, as you write, you will decide to change the ending; the path taken by the script may need to be changed and refocused on some other climax. Make the change only if it is your reasoned determination, not something that happened because your plot got out of control.

If you have written an outline or treatment (see chapter 2), you can work directly from it. Use it as your framework to build on. It will keep you from straying, setting you firmly on the path that leads inevitably, but never predictably, to your predetermined climax. Outlines and treatments are always written in the present tense. (See chapter 7, excerpt from a treatment for *Kingdom in the Dust* by Isabelle Ziegler.)

SCRIPT DIVISIONS

After planning your teleplay, divide your script into three acts. (Whatever you do, at this point do not concern yourself about the breaks in the script that are necessitated by commercial breaks. These are determined after purchase when the shooting script is being prepared.)

The following diagram illustrates how to divide your script into three acts:

ACT I	ACT II	ACT III
Problem or Conflict Introduced (Approx. ¼ of script)	Conflict between protagonist and antagonist leading to ↓ (Approx. ½ of script) the seemingly unsolvable problem	Action providing solution to the conflict (Final ¼ of the script)

After the basic plot is established, either in your mind or on paper, divide your story into those three acts. If they are not clear to you, then you need to rework the elements of your story until they fall into the three-act structure. Determine what you want to say in each act and how each will rise to a crisis that will propel the plot forward. Each act must build to a point of dramatic impact (as forceful as a knife thrown into a man's back or as delicate as a woman's laughter suddenly turning into tears) in which the viewer is totally absorbed.

All action in the first two acts leads into and away from the seemingly unsolvable problem, which usually occurs about three-fourths of the way through the script.

The seemingly unsolvable problem occurs at the point when the protagonist(s) are caught in a web of circumstances that you have woven around them from the beginning and from which they long to escape but cannot (or so it seems).

Example: Two children run away from a home in which they are mistreated by their parents. After many misadventures they are taken in and cared for by a kindly old man who unwittingly lets the juvenile authorities know where they are. They are returned home where their sadistic alcoholic parents await them. They cannot run away again because they are locked in, the kindly old man is lost to them, and the authorities, unaware of the true situation, have dismissed them. There is no escape; their problem seems unsolvable. You must now find a solution, one that rises to the inevitable climax, but it must not be forced or made to occur through some miracle. It must come from your characters themselves (perhaps a weakening on the part of one parent), yet must also be something that has already been suggested or implied through skillful exposition.

The major problem or conflict has been stated during the first few pages, the first minutes of the teleplay, and from there the plot rises in a series of crises, through the unsolvable problem, to the climax, which comes at or near the end. To understand this, study the dramatic teleplays on your home screen and in the film scripts which you have obtained from the publishers listed in chapter 6.

In an open-ended series (daytime serials and the mini-series—a teleplay presented in several weekly segments) this construction is also valid despite the fact that there is no *ultimate* climax until the end of the serial. Each script should have a provocative opening, build interest through some conflict or problem, and end on an up-beat (cliff-hanging) note.

Don't confuse the basic three-act plot structure with the commercial breaks, which are more numerous and are also called "acts" simply because the word is a holdover from live plays. Hold to your three-act structure; it is necessary for a strong dramatic framework. (See chapter 4 for explanation of commercial breaks.)

IMITATION AND SYMBOLISM

Symbolism is a statement within a statement. The young girl in a white dress, holding a bouquet of daisies, is a symbol of innocence. She is also a visual cliché. There is really little time in teleplays, except for the 120-minute shows, for the use of symbolism. The viewers are too absorbed in the drama to wonder, what is the real meaning of that? The plot is the thing; don't inject a lot of obscure symbolism that will detract from it.

Avoid the temptation to write imitations of the successful teleplays you admire, whether you are writing a movie for television, a pilot for an original series, or a script for an established program. Don't be a copycat. Originality is a much valued and sought-after commodity in television, so no matter how enthusiastic you are about a particular show, don't produce a secondhand version of it.

If you are writing for a series, of course, you must keep your script within that particular program's format and use the same characters, settings, and theme. But there are hundreds of variations within these limitations.

Consider the many kinds of programs from which you may choose. (See chapter 3 for information on the *Television Market List,* which includes all current continuing programs with the exception of daytime serials.)

CHARACTERIZATION

All teleplays are concerned with human beings, how they act and the consequences of their actions. For the duration of the teleplay they must always be persons about whom the viewer really cares. Whether one regards them with affection or disdain, they must be real and interesting. They must elicit a feeling of empathy or some definite emotional reaction. We are speaking of the principal characters and the important supporting players. Secondary characters must be kept at a minimum because there simply is not enough time to develop strong minor characters. Even in the 120-minute teleplays they are portrayed principally through some outstanding and distinguishing characteristic.

Know your principal characters as you know yourself. Study your characters as if you were a psychologist—and good writers are, by nature, fairly good psychologists. Know their occupations, motivations, habits, fears, joys, prejudices, vices, how they walk and dress and talk. If you are writing for an established series, the research and development of the characters has been done for you, but you must understand them as thoroughly as if they were your own creations.

Carefully build the conflict between the protagonist and the antagonist, making the villain an opponent worthy of the hero. At the climax, it must be clear that they have fought their best fight, regardless of the outcome. Your antagonist need not be another human being. It can be a force of nature, such as a hurricane, tornado, earthquake; it can be a political system, such as a despotic dictatorship or some other form of suppressive society.

STEREOTYPES

Don't be lazy and use characters created by other writers (unless you are writing for a series, of course). Forget about such stock favorites as the mousy librarian, the absent-minded professor, the mindless macho truck driver, the whore-with-the-heart-of-gold. They have been written about so often that you may think it is safe to use them. Don't do it. Stop thinking in terms of cliché characters, unless you are writing a parody based on stereotypes. Every human being is unique; portray him/her as such.

Suppose you have two brothers who on the surface seem to be the same man. They are both bankers, both stuffy, both ultra conservative. Yet one plays jazz guitar and follows the horses from Santa Anita to Churchill Downs; the other is a mime of almost professional talent and takes two weeks off every six months to stay roaring drunk. Once you get under their skins, each will come to life. As for that mindless macho truck driver, he grows prize dahlias and is depressed for days after his 2-ton runs over a rabbit in the road.

MOTIVATION

The reason for a character's behavior is his motivation. In the course of your teleplay it will be necessary for your protagonist to undergo philosophical and/or emotional changes and for you to give reasons for them that the viewer will understand; these often spring from some confrontation with the antagonist. There should be surprises for the viewers but none which do not, after the fact, have completely logical explanations. Both protagonist and antagonist must act and react in a manner that is understood, as should any other character who is important to the drama. In *The Rookies* teleplay *Blue Christmas,* written by Aaron Spelling, an apparently frightened elderly woman calls the police to report a prowler. The Rookies respond to the call and, during their investigation, realize that there was no prowler and that her call was motivated by the pain of loneliness and a desperate need for companionship on Christmas Eve. (See excerpt from *The Rookies* in chapter 7.)

CONSISTENCY

A human being declares himself through what he does and says. In your teleplay your characters must reveal their inner selves in such a way that what they do and say is entirely consistent with the characters you have given them. In their dialog, for instance, you cannot have a fifth-grade dropout speaking in the well-honed phrases of, say, Gore Vidal. Such inconsistency would be ludicrous. As for their behavior, you can have a basically selfish individual perform an act of generosity if it is consistent with his character. For instance, in *All in the Family* Archie Bunker's stinginess and his dislike for his son-in-law, Mike, are both well established. Yet, without any encouragement, Archie offers to pay for Mike's appendectomy. This is totally consistent with Archie's character since it is motivated by his desire to alleviate the anxiety of the daughter he loves so much.

CONTRASTS

Contrasts provide drama, and the tensile interplay between characters depends heavily upon them. All characters, even within a family unit, must have apparent differences, both physical and psychological, however subtle. Your protagonist and antagonist must have more emphatic contrasts, yet they do not need to be poles apart. For example, both may be cattle barons or bank robbers. But the kinds of men they are must be molded from different clay: these differences will spark the conflict on which your plot is structured. Suppose you have two sisters, one strong and one weak. The strong one, the antagonist, is destroying her family through rampant venality and selfishness. The weak one passively allows it to continue until some diabolic action by her sister sparks her determination to fight back. The two women look alike, talk alike, even live in the same house, but there is an enormous psychological difference between them.

ENVIRONMENT

Carefully research the environment in which you have set your plot. No human being is totally molded by his or her environment, yet none remains untouched by it—whether it is the Arizona Territory in 1850 or a city ghetto in the 1970s. It may be a place for transients, such as a resort on the Italian Riviera, to which none of your characters is native but which still has some impact upon them and their behavior.

Time is important to environment, too, whether it is the late 1970s *(Executive Suite)* or the 1870s *(Wild Wild West).* Any period earlier than 1960 should be researched for customs, social mores and behavior, modes of dress, and so on. Be at home in your environment because, until your teleplay is finished, all your working hours will be spent there.

CHARACTER EXPOSITION

Your characters must be exposed through dialog, behavior, and appearance. This is a form of exposition (revealing the facts) which shows exactly what manner of man/woman the character really is. You must know precisely how they talk (their vocabularies, idiom, slang, and what makes them whisper, yell, or whine).

Good characterization will depend upon the inner lives you have given your characters. Deliver them to the viewer as you want them to be seen and understood—whether they are violent or passive, brutal or compassionate.

Appearances are revealing, too. If it is a costume teleplay, the costumes must be studiously researched, but clothes in contemporary America are also costumes. A New Jersey dockworker does not dress like a Los Angeles swinger, nor a Mississippi redneck like a television anchorman.

DIALOG

Motion pictures are primarily a visual medium; television is a verbal medium. Your ear for dialog must be finely tuned because it is through dialog that your characters will come to life and the plot will develop. Occasionally some action will take the center of the small screen, but it is principally through dialog that the drama will unfold.

PURPOSE

Every word of dialog must count for something, whether to: (1) *present an immediate problem,* (2) *reveal the characters,* (3) *advance the plot,* or (4) *provide exposition.*

Presentation of Problem. An example of dialog that presents an immediate problem is from the *Phyllis* teleplay *You're Not Getting Better, Just Older* (written by David Lloyd), in which Phyllis is facing her forty-fifth birthday:

> AUDREY
>
> That's right! Instead of moaning
>
> about your birthday why don't you
>
> <u>celebrate</u> it?
>
> MOTHER DEXTER
>
> Give a party! Laugh . . . sing . . .
>
> get it on. . . .
>
> PHYLLIS
>
> What a wonderful idea! And
>
> how typical of you, my dear
>
> good friends, to think of it
>
> in order to cheer me when I'm
>
> feeling low. I'll do it.
>
> I'll give a party - you'll
>
> come, won't you, Jonathan?

                    JONATHAN

          I'm sorry, Phyllis. But I have

          a meeting that night.

                    PHYLLIS

          Audrey?

                    AUDREY

          I'm afraid I promised to visit

          my sister.

PHYLLIS LOOKS AT MOTHER DEXTER

                    MOTHER DEXTER

          Aren't you going to invite me?

                    PHYLLIS

          Well, I just assumed you wouldn't

          be interested in coming.

                    MOTHER DEXTER

          Why would you assume that, dear?

                    PHYLLIS

          Well, I just assumed that you

          would have other plans.

                    MOTHER DEXTER

          I have no other plans.

                          PHYLLIS

          Then you'll come?

                      MOTHER DEXTER

          To your birthday party? I'd

          rather have a root canal.

   Now we know, given Phyllis's egocentric nature, that how and
with whom she will celebrate her birthday is the immediate problem,
the one on which all subsequent action will be focused.

   Revelation of Character. An example of dialog that reveals the
character is from a *Rhoda* teleplay, *Myrna's Story,* written by Linda
Bloodworth:

                          BRENDA

          . . . You know, cute has a definite

          place in business. I mean, even

          at the bank all the guys flirt . . .

          I hear tell.

                           RHODA

          Do me a favor. I've got a lot

          to do right now, and I can't

          deal with this. Stop putting

          yourself down.

BRENDA

I'm just telling the truth.

All the best looking girls

start out in the new accounts

department. Y'know . . . right

out front in the first window . . .

where everybody sees them.

You want to put your money

in that bank when you walk

in there and see that pretty

face. . . . Do you want to know

where they started me?

RHODA

No.

BRENDA

Go ahead, ask me. I'll give

you a hint. It wasn't new

accounts.

RHODA

Brenda, I don't want to know.

BRENDA

In the vault . . . rolling dimes.

From this dialog much is learned about Rhoda's sister, Brenda— her wit, her self-mockery, her pessimistic view of herself as a desirable female. This is consistent with Brenda's established character, of course.

Plot Advancement. An example of dialog that advances the plot is from the second draft of *The Godfather,* by Mario Puzo, in which, after struggling against making the decision, Michael has finally chosen to join "The Family" and devote his life to organized crime:

MICHAEL
It's all personal. Every piece of
shit a man has to eat every day of
his life is personal. You know
where I learned that from? My
father. The Don. The Godfather.
If a bolt of lightning hit a friend
of his, my old man would take it
personal. He took my going into
the Marines personal. He takes
everything personal. That's what
makes him the great Don. He knows
every feather that falls from the
tail of a sparrow or however the
hell that goes. Okay, I'm coming
late but I'm coming all the way.
Damn right I take this busted jaw
personal. Damn right I take
Sollozzo shooting my father
personal.
(Long pause)
You know, I can never remember my
father hitting me or my brothers,
or even yelling at Connie. And
tell the truth, Tom, how many men
do you figure the Don killed or
had killed?

From this turning point, now that his painful decision has been made, we know that Michael has undergone a philosophical change and will move against the old Don's enemies, with the inevitable violent results.

Exposition. Exposition is the exposure of facts and/or ideas. Unlike the novelist, the television writer cannot simply disclose in the narration what has gone on before. Exposition is used in the teleplay to tell what has happened, either before a particular scene or before the teleplay itself began. With one exception, it is always done through dialog. The exception is the use of a narrator who, as the film fades in, explains the events that led up to the present situation. Unless you are writing an epic to be produced as a serial in several parts, you would seldom use this device. It is too reminiscent of the theatrical cliché, the butler-maid dialog in the opening moments of a stage play that sets the scene for the audience. In such dialog, for example, we would be told that Young Master Edward broke his leg playing cricket, that Lady Widenham is recovering from a stroke brought about by the theft of her emerald necklace, that her nephew Mr. Bumpsie has just arrived on a furlough from India, that Miss Edwina's engagement to Sir Clarence is off, and that they suspect the reason for it is Mr. Dabney, the new young vicar. All of this provides us with sufficient clues to previous events so that no further background explanations (exposition) are necessary when the characters finally appear on stage.

Skillful exposition is so smoothly injected into a teleplay that the viewers are unaware they are being fed hard facts. This calls for much subtlety, inventiveness, and imagination on your part. Never deliver facts so that they seem to be dragged in, such as a character's monolog describing previous events or a scene in which your only purpose is to establish a single fact.

An example of dialog that provides exposition (explanation of exposition follows) is in the following scene from *Eleanor and Franklin,* screenplay by James Costigan from the book by Joseph P. Lash, *Eleanor and Franklin:*

MED CLOSE SHOT

>   ELEANOR
> You said that only a moment before
> he fainted you looked over to see him
> smiling at someone. At whom?

FULL SHOT

over Eleanor's back in f.g. favors reacting
Laura center b.g.

>   ELEANOR
> At Daisy? At Madame Shoumatoff?

>   LAURA
> No. No!

>   ELEANOR
> Who else was in the room?

>   LAURA
> Must I say?

>   ELEANOR
> No. Not if you don't want to.

FULL SHOT

over back of Eleanor r.f.g. favors Laura moving
toward Eleanor.

>   LAURA
>   (sighing)
> Well . . . it's bound to come out,
> one way or another. Mrs. Rutherfurd
> was here.

>   ELEANOR
> Mrs. Rutherfurd?

>   LAURA
> Lucy.

CLOSE SHOT

reacting Eleanor looks o.s.l.*

> LAURA
> You remember, she used to be Lucy
> Mercer. Married old Wintie Ruther-
> furd. Uh he, died not too long ago.

> ELEANOR
> And they started seeing one another
> again . . . she and Franklin? She came
> down here to visit him?

This dialog exposes these facts: (1) there was another woman with Franklin when he died, a woman whose presence Eleanor had not suspected; (2) the woman, a Mrs. Rutherfurd, was previously known to Eleanor as Lucy Mercer when Franklin and Lucy had been seeing each other years ago; and (3) Eleanor did not know that their relationship had been resumed. As Eleanor receives these facts, so do the viewers.

Ernest Lehman, successful writer-producer-director, says, "I think a bit of advice I would give (to aspiring writers), whether it is needed or not, is: be aware of the difficulties of conveying exposition. Try to spoon-feed exposition in such a way that it is palatable, so that it doesn't *seem* to be exposition. Try to work it into a scene that has a little bit of conflict so that the character seems to be forced to say what he's saying, rather than conveniently saying it to achieve the writer's end."

Be stealthy about your exposition. Sneak it in so that it becomes fact before the audience is aware of it.

To learn how exposition is handled by the masters, read the plays written by the great playwrights, living and dead. You will find them in your local library. Among the moderns, perhaps the best examples can be found in the works of Arthur Miller, Tennessee Williams, William Inge, Paddy Chayevsky, and Neil Simon.

---

*o.s.l. is the abbreviation for off-screen left.

"Natural" Dialog

There is a difference between dialog that *is* natural and dialog that *seems* natural. You are striving for the latter. It is almost impossible to duplicate actual conversation, which would ramble and waste too much time on irrelevancies, becoming both boring and confusing. It would be flip-the-dial time. Never attempt to write group dialog as it really sounds when several people are gathered together. The result is a garbled noise with no single voice predominant. There can be a murmur of voices in the background, but one or two voices must be distinctly heard by the viewer. This may not seem like reality to you but it is dramatic reality.

Again, people do ramble when they speak together but should not ramble in your teleplay. Keep the dialog moving.

Wherever you go, as you move around in your life, study the way people speak. Tune in to the nuances and speech patterns of various groups. If you have, say, three men in a scene—a priest, a drug pusher, a policeman—it should be clear to the viewer with his eyes closed which of the three is speaking, not only from what each says but from his choice of words.

Human speech does not flow smoothly from the lips, even among college professors and politicians. It is often fragmented. There are "uh's" and "ah's," pauses and sighs. There are groans and moans and whistles and gasps that speak volumes. Use them when they are appropriate. In many instances they serve better than a full sentence, are more provocative, and give greater impetus to the dialog.

Remember that your characters are visible, so it is unnecessary and unnatural for them to call each other frequently by name. This device is a throwback to the old days of radio when it was necessary to let the listeners know who was in the scene, so that there was a lot of dialog with "Well, Mary," "All right, Clyde," and so on, in it. You don't need this for television.

What the characters do *not* say can often have more significance than several lines of dialog. If a talkative character suddenly becomes mute, his silence can be golden so far as the dramatic effect is concerned.

TEMPO

Dialog requires changes of tempo, which are achieved by pacing it with long, short, and staccato passages. This means scenes in which the characters have long speeches interspersed with short speeches or brief bursts of speech. But they must fall into place naturally, never seeming forced.

Ideally, the dialog should be written so that it requires no parenthetical directions. Before a character's dialog it should not be necessary to write (slowly) or (thoughtfully) or (angrily). That should be implicit in the dialog itself. However, if you feel that the line is open to several interpretations, by all means use the parenthetical direction.

Avoid lengthy monologs. Reality does not allow for them, regardless of their literary or poetic brilliance. Also, this is a sloppy effort to get into a character's mind and expose his inner monolog to the viewer. Whatever is in his mind must be revealed through some other means—an exchange of dialog with another character or some action that illuminates it.

Never present a character who is one kind of person and have him/her speak like another.

Example:

Two men meet in the hallway of a tenement building.

JUNKIE
Will you please sell me five
dollars worth of heroin?

DEALER
I don't have it and if I did I
wouldn't sell it to you. There
are too many policemen around.

These men would never address each other in that manner. Their speech is much too formal, too ordinary. It might go like this:

```
                      JUNKIE
         Hey, man, I gotta have some smack
         - gimme a nickel bag.

                      DEALER
         Scag, hell. The Man dried it up.
```

This is an exaggerated example but it shows how important, both to character delineation and to dialog vitality, it is to make certain the characters speak from their essential personalities.

Never use a word that your characters would not use. And never use one that doesn't say exactly what you mean for it to say. Don't settle for second best.

The BBC production *Upstairs, Downstairs* offers splendid examples of the precision demanded in dialog among characters who occupy various social and economic levels. Mr. Hudson, the autocratic butler, uses words and phrases which are typically his and would never be used by Ruby, the scullery maid.

CLICHÉS

Clichés in dialog are to be avoided as assiduously as stereotypes in characters. The exception is when you have circumstances in which characters actually tend to speak in clichés. The small-town druggist may actually greet a customer with, "Is it hot enough for you?" An innocent young boy, in the throes of first love, may actually say to his girl, "Your eyes are like the stars." But unless this is the way your characters would naturally speak, and so reveals something about them, their dialog should never slip into the lifelessness of clichés.

NARRATIVE

Narrative is the description of the setting, characters, and/or action which follows the shot designation and precedes or follows the dialog. All sound effects are written into the narrative, as are all stage directions.

An example of how narrative is used following the shot designation and between the dialog of two characters is seen in *The Rookies* teleplay *Blue Christmas:*

```
INT. BAR - NIGHT

It is a typical neighborhood racially-mixed
bar, with bowling decor . . . few tables, booths.
Christmas lights are on behind the bar. The bar
is fairly crowded and all the customers are
backed into a corner, watching SAM REECE flip
his lid. Debris is all over the place and Sam, a
black man in his fifties, heavyset, has a broken
whiskey bottle clutched in his hand. MURPHY, a
very frightened bartender-owner, is cowering by
the front door, runs to Terry and Chris as they
enter, size up the scene.

                    MURPHY
          He's crazy! The guy's crazy!

                    TERRY
          What happened?

                    MURPHY
          Nothing! He was drinking -
          minding his own business -
          suddenly he just got up, started
          throwing things.

                    TERRY
          Do you know him?

                    MURPHY
          Never saw him before.

Terry nods to Chris. They unsnap their holsters,
separate, slowly move toward the man at
different angles.

                    TERRY
                 (quietly)
          Okay, drop the bottle.
```

The narrative contains only what the camera can actually record. Never describe what occurs in a character's mind unless it can be shown on the screen.

You don't have the latitude in script writing that you do in novel writing. Never describe action that will not be seen or heard by the audience.

You would not write: "Jamie has just been reprimanded by his mother, and thinks, 'I am going to run away from home.' " It would be impossible to photograph his inner monolog. What he thinks would have to be presented through subsequent dialog or action. (An exception to this rule is the occasional expository comment that is written into the narrative.)

Sometimes it is necessary to explain to the director exactly how you visualize a scene. You might feel it is important to remind the director that a certain character has a peculiar handicap. You would write, "Keep in mind that Mamie can neither read nor write."

The first time each character appears in the narrative, he/she should be briefly described. This description should contain elements of both physical appearance and character.

Example: "George X is a short rotund man with an overbearing and obnoxious personality." Ordinarily you would not need to explain that George X is short and rotund except that, in this instance, it is important to both his character and its development since his short stature is responsible for his belligerence. In physical descriptions do not simply write, "He is tall, ruggedly handsome, with curly blond hair." This has nothing to do with the *kind* of character he is. Also, it places limits on the number of actors who could play the role.

Your narrative prose need not be brilliantly written—it can even be written in incomplete sentences. But it must be clear, concise, and always in the *present tense*.

2

How to Develop the Teleplay

Your teleplay now has a plot sketched in with conflict, characters, crises, and the climax. You have written voluminous notes and are ready to bring them together in a cohesive dramatic structure. Your first burning question is: How do I effectively translate all of these components into a teleplay? Your second is: How do I put on paper what my mind's eye sees and what must be clearly shown to the potential buyers of my teleplay—and ultimately to the viewers?

First comes organization. All those ideas that are tumbling around in your mind must be separated, put into order, and brought into focus.

ORGANIZATION

It is a good idea to begin by writing a treatment or outline of your story.

A treatment is the scene-by-scene narrative of your entire story written in the present tense. Unlike the outline, it contains more details than just the characters, locale, scenes, crises, and climax. In a treatment you will include act breaks, selective dialog that provides certain character exposition, and some camera directions.

A treatment can vary in length from 15 to 45 pages; the subject matter will dictate its length. In it you tell the story as if you were telling it to a friend: what happens, what happens next. Since you may decide to submit it either with your complete script or by itself, it must be as gripping and as innovative as you can make it. Hook the reader on the first page. Remember that agents and potential buyers have mountains of scripts to read and they will probably be most inspired to concentrate on the provocative ones. (See excerpt from treatment for *Kingdom in the Dust,* by Isabelle Ziegler, in chapter 7.)

An outline is shorter than a treatment, usually about 7 to 15 pages. Because of its brevity, it cannot include all scenes, only the major ones. Introduce all important characters and, if you like, include some dialog. The protagonist must be made interesting immediately and the conflict/problem clearly stated within the first page or two. Like the treatment, the outline is written in the present tense. Don't underestimate the importance of a well-written outline. It is not impossible that a strong thematic teleplay, such as *The Waltons,* would be bought from an outline.

If you submit only the treatment or outline and it is turned over to another writer to write or to develop, you will receive much less money than you would for the complete script. It is important at this stage in your career to go all out and write the entire script. Also, it is very important to your screen credits. On the screen your credit will read: "Written by John Doe," which is much more prestigious than: "Story by John Doe—written by Jane Moe." Producers notice these credits, and they can be extremely helpful in opening up the television market for you.

The outline will serve as the skeleton of your teleplay as you now begin to block in its many scenes.

One technique for organizing scenes is the use of lined 3 x 5 index cards. Write each scene on a card, along with salient fragments of action or dialog that pertain to it. On each card, as you introduce a new character or scene, jot down a brief description of the person or place. Later these scenes will be filled out and fully developed as you work out the most minute details of your teleplay—word by word.

Tack the cards on a cork board in the sequence that seems logical to you, probably dividing them by scenes as you believe they will fall under the three acts.

Instead of index cards you may use a blackboard or legal pads or notebooks, but if your plot is convoluted in design, the index cards are easier to rearrange. For instance, suppose you have a respectable citizen who is an ex-convict, when do you disclose this information for its maximum theatrical effect? Write it on a card and move it around among the other scenes until you find its most effective slot.

THREE ACTS

Refer to the diagram in chapter 1 (p. 4) which shows how the teleplay is divided into three acts. In some scripts these acts are designated; in others they are not. (Specifics follow in chapter 4.) But always have them firmly in mind to facilitate your plot structuring.

Act 1—the conflict or action that rises to to a crisis or sets up the sharp confrontation in ACT 2.

Act 2—the actions which end with the hero/heroine caught in what seems an unsolvable problem.

Act 3—the resolution of all conflicts, rising to the inevitable climax.

A good way to divide the acts into lengths that best serve a well-constructed plot is: ACT I, approximately one-fourth of the total length; ACT II, approximately one-half of the total; and ACT III, approximately one-fourth of the total. "Approximately" means just that; these divisions can be anywhere from one to several pages off the mark. However, when you time the acts of teleplays you will discover that they invariably hold true, give or take a minute or two.

The three-act structure is elemental to plot construction. Do not confuse this basic dramatic technique, which is indispensable to correct plotting, with the four or more acts that are used in teleplays. These teleplay act divisions function solely to accommodate commercial breaks. Use the three-act structure to develop your script.

After your script is completed, check the format of the show for which you are writing in order to divide the material into that specific format. Your script is salable, however, without designating these act divisions. (The movie for television should follow the screenwriting script format.)

QUESTIONS TO BE ANSWERED

Now is the time to ask yourself:

Is my protagonist interesting; will the viewers really care about him/her? Does he make events happen (as he should) or is he passive? Is my antagonist worthy of the protagonist? Will the readers (the potential buyers) be intrigued by my script within the first 5 to 10 pages? Is my opening scene so provocative that they cannot refrain from reading more? Does it serve as a compelling lead-in to the major conflict/problem that besets my characters? Have I built the plot carefully on the cards and in the treatment or outline so that I know exactly where it is going—exactly what the climax is? Have I clearly presented the conflict/problem within the first 5 pages?

If all these questions receive affirmative answers, you can feel fairly confident that you are working on a probable winner. If there are any negative answers or questions about them, rework them immediately. Don't count on remedying them as you go along. Never leave anything to happy chance.

TELEPLAY STYLES

There are two styles in which teleplays are written—the *shot-by-shot* technique, which is the most acceptable; and the *master scene* technique. Some writers use both in a single script where they best serve the visual content. You may use either technique to the exclusion of the other if it works best for the script; but if you decide to combine them, do so with caution. Don't jumble them so that the script becomes confusing. There is no single way to write a script, but it must be visually precise. Ernest Lehman says, "I want it written with clarity so that the director, actors, and so forth know what is intended." The key to excellence in any kind of filmwriting: what is intended must be *clearly* stated.

SHOT-BY-SHOT TECHNIQUE

Basically film is composed of several thousand feet of frames, which are spliced, edited, and run on reels to make the moving pictures. A frame is the rectangle which the camera discloses, similar to a snapshot. It has definite boundaries. These frames are also referred to as shots. You must be able to visualize your story scene by scene and, within each scene, shot by shot. Above all, be able to identify the *subject* of each shot.

The shot-by-shot technique is a form of filmwriting that is done in a clear, unencumbered style. It enables a reader to grasp easily the content of the script by following the capitalized shots, without having to rely solely on the narrative or dialog. *A shot is the specific picture on the screen.* Whether written in the shot-by-shot technique or in master scenes, films are always made in shots (see excerpt from *The Rookies* in chapter 7).

Do not number the shots in your script. Some writers do this, but we feel that it adds nothing to the reader's knowledge and, in any event, the script will not be filmed exactly as the shot numbers indicate. (The shots are numbered in *The Rookies* because it is a revised final draft of the script.)

The subject of the shot is the object on which the camera is focused. It can be an Indian on horseback, a couple lying on the beach, a dog, a signpost—anything that dominates the shot and on which the viewer is meant to concentrate. It is identified in capital letters and followed either by dialog or by the narrative describing the action that takes place in the scene. Whenever the camera moves to focus on something different—setting, object, actor, whatever— it must be clearly identified as a new shot. This makes the instruction CUT TO unnecessary since the camera must cut to or move with each new shot identified.

Remember that a camera shot is similar to an Instamatic snapshot. Suppose you snap a shot of CINDERELLA scrubbing the floor while her stepmother and two stepsisters are sipping tea in b.g. In your script it would be written this way, followed by the descriptive narrative:

CINDERELLA

On her knees before her fireplace scrubbing
hearth. She is crying. In b.g. we see her
stepmother and stepsisters GIGGLING and sipping
tea.

We noted that there is no need for the instruction CUT TO. Though the actual instruction is seldom written into the script (unless you are writing a master scene), the ability of a camera to cut from one shot to another is one of the most valuable techniques of filmwriting and filmmaking. It gives the film great forward mobility, moving the action along swiftly and smoothly at an agreeable pace. The novice screenwriter must learn *not* to bore the reader or producer by following an idea, step by tedious step, from its origin to its conclusion—such as taking a character from one location to another while the camera is trained upon him. For instance, it is not necessary to follow a character into a building, across the lobby, into the elevator, down a hall, and into an office. This would be indicated by: EXT. DAY-BUILDING, followed by INT. OFFICE.

Example: A boy asks a girl to go to a prom. In the next shot we CUT TO a dress shop where she is standing before a mirror admiring a formal dress. In the next shot the boy is admiring the same dress when she opens her door to greet him. Today's sophisticated audiences always understand that DISSOLVE means the end of one scene or a change of time or both. Study the excerpts from *The Rookies* in chapter 7 for shot changes within a single scene.

After you have chosen the subject of the camera shot, you must indicate whether the setting is inside or outside and whether it is day or night. This is written:
EXT. - DAY

INT. - NIGHT

You may, of course, use other designations for night or day if they are important to the mood—such as dawn, dusk, and so on. If it is obvious in the script that the shots following the original designation are taken at the same time, there is no need to repeat the instructions.

MASTER SCENE TECHNIQUE

A master scene is one in which all narrative, dialog, and action relative to a single setting/place is written beneath the initial description of the locale. There are times when you simply will not be able to break it into specific subjects of the shots; too much is going on simultaneously. Within a single scene there may be several interesting camera angles or cuts, but you do not write them. That is left to the director when he works with you or another writer on the final shooting script.

Remember the difference between a scene and a shot: a scene includes all action and dialog that occurs in one locale; a shot is similar to a snapshot, and many shots may be incorporated in a single scene.

The following is a good example of a master scene in which you will see that there is so much action within the single machine shop scene, so much happening simultaneously, that it would be impossible to write it in the shot-by-shot technique. Note that in addition to action, it includes snatches of dialog that are vital to the exposition. (Written by Constance Nash for this book.)

```
INT. MACHINE SHOP - LEWISBURG PENITENTIARY

The SOUND of a tool-and-die machine is WHIRRING
above the noise of an argument between TONY LUCA
and ERNIE. Looking on, standing next to them,
are TWO PRISONERS.

TWO GUARDS standing about 10 feet from the
machine are engrossed in a conversation. They
are unaware of the fight.
                                        (CONTINUED)
```

ANOTHER GROUP of prisoners are keeping a wary eye on the potentially explosive scene. They continue with their work taking sly glances at the potentially serious fight.

THE GUARDS are now laughing. One, a tall, military-looking type, is making an obscene gesture with his right hand. The other guard, shorter and stockier, is laughing harder now.

We CUT TO a medium shot of TONY LUCA, his face etched in stolid anger, jaws clamped. He looks like a coiled snake who is evaluating just when to strike. The two prisoners, LEO and SAMMY, seem to be encouraging the showdown.

ERNIE, a wiry, tough Italian, is ready to attack Luca any minute now. He is standing with legs spread, arms out, clutching a mean-looking wrench poised at just the right angle to bring down on Luca's head.

> LEO
> (tauntingly quiet)
> Yeh, baby. Let pretty boy have
> it.

Luca is cornered. He looks as if he would like to kill Ernie but all he has are his hands.

> ERNIE
> Come on . . . you don't have nobody
> here from the Family to wipe yur
> nose . . . that's right . . . a little
> closer.

Ernie is gesturing with his hands, taunting Luca to come closer. Ernie has a devilish grin.

(CONTINUED)

                    LUCA
          Put the club down. You never could
          fight like a man. (He spits.)
          Chicken-livered pansy.

THE GUARDS glance beyond the tool-and-die
machine, checking the larger group of men who
are supposedly working hard. Everything looks
cool. They turn their backs, not hearing the
words between Luca and Ernie.

ONE BLACK DUDE from the other group slides over
slowly, very slowly, toward Luca and Ernie. He
has a file in his hand. We see a CLOSE-UP of the
FILE slipping up his denim shirt sleeve. LEO
notices, keeping his eyes riveted on the black
guy who joins them.

Ernie knows there are two things an Italian man
isn't: a fag or a drunk. He hates Luca now.

                    LEO
          Did ya hear him? Pretty boy
          says ya ain't a man.

                  BLACK PRISONER
               (under his breath)
          Shut up!

ERNIE springs, his wrench CRACKS across Luca's
skull. There is a deadening thud as blood spurts
out like a hose that springs a leak. Luca
grapples with Ernie, both falling down.

The BLACK PRISONER sticks his file into Luca's
hand. Luca is dazed. The three men steal anxious
glances around the machine shop toward the
guards.
                              (CONTINUED)

CONTINUED:

The stocky guard stops laughing. Strains to
listen.

ERNIE batters LUCA mercilessly. Luca, as a final
move to defend himself, stabs the lethal file
into Ernie's neck. It is a lucky hit. Ernie gags
and moans.

Luca is lying in a pool of blood, his face all but
unrecognizable.

                    TALL GUARD
                   (yelling)
          What's going on over there? Hey!

The GUARDS ring for assistance, and run down to
Ernie and Luca. Their faces are grim and
suddenly mean-looking. They stand over the
scene, incredulous. (beat) The SHORT GUARD
heads for the phone.

TERMINOLOGY

Every craft, sport, trade, and profession develops its own particular terminology, which becomes essential for quick communication among those who participate in it. It is vital to your understanding of how to write a teleplay that you study and become thoroughly familiar with the terms given below before you tackle your rough (first) draft. Otherwise you cannot hope to bring your teleplay to its complete visual realization.

You cannot understand these terms merely by memorizing them; you must work with them. Remember that it is the mark of the amateur to overuse or incorrectly use camera directions and editing techniques. These decisions must be left to the director.

There are times in every teleplay when it is imperative to designate certain shots, such as POV, CLOSE-UP, or PAN, to give dramatic definition to a particular scene. This defines the specific meaning or intention of the scene to the producer and the director.

As an example of a CLOSE-UP shot, you might need to show, for dramatic impact, exactly the way in which two men shake hands. It could be a perfunctory shake but it is not, so you write:

CLOSE-UP—HANDS TIGHTLY GRIPPED

Beginning teleplay writers are either frightened by camera instructions and refuse to use them, or enamored of them and use them to excess. If you know how to use the terms properly, you won't be guilty of either mistake.

One last warning: unless the directions are absolutely vital to the director's understanding of the explicit intent of the scene, avoid "directing on paper."

The teleplay vocabulary can be broken into five general categories: (1) *Camera Angle Descriptions*—terms that designate the position and angle of the camera in relation to its subject. (2) *Special Effects Shots*—an aptly named category that includes the terms needed for camera and editing techniques which provide heightened dramatic effects. (3) *Transitional Instructions*—terms that show how one scene is DISSOLVED or CUT TO another scene. (4) *Subject-in-Motion Shots*—terms to indicate whether the camera is stationary or in motion when the subject of the shot is moving. (5) *Audio Instructions*—terms used to inject special sound effects into the script.

There are other terms which defy categorizing but with which you will also need to become familiar. These are:

FRAME: A rectangle which the camera discloses, similar to a snapshot; has definite boundaries. A 5-inch strip of film would have several frames.

SHOT: The specific picture on the screen, interchangeable with the term "frame." Specifically the shot is the picture within the frame.

INTO VIEW: Used when the shot first reveals another portion of the whole and slowly moves to include the rest of the subject. Example: Two people are in bed. First the camera focuses on the wife, then moves to her husband. The directions would read: HUSBAND INTO VIEW. The camera brings INTO

VIEW the rest of the subject of the shot. The subject of the shot would be: INT.-NIGHT-BEDROOM. (INTO FRAME means that something enters the shot/scene on which the camera is already focused. Example: When the camera is focused on the woman in bed, her husband is not lying beside her. He comes INTO FRAME from off screen. It does not bring the husband INTO VIEW; it simply lets something new into the original shot.)

b.g. (abbreviation of background): Used within the narrative and described in lower-case initials. It refers to something happening in the background of the shot while attention is focused on the foreground. Example: Two people are lying on the deck of a small boat. In the b.g. we see a large boat bearing down upon them. (You may always write the entire word if you prefer.)

PAUSE and BEAT: Used to mark a pause in dialog. You can break a character's long speech by inserting (BEAT) or (PAUSE).

CONTINUED: Written under a character's name when his dialog has been interrupted by some action (not by another character speaking) and is continued. Also used in the script when the dialog or scene is continued on the next page. See Chapter 7 for examples.

PARENTHETICAL DIRECTIONS: Directions showing how a line is to be delivered or what the character is doing. These appear beneath the character's name, preceding his dialog. They are very brief, so minimal that it is not necessary to make of them a separate narrative passage. They are used only when needed to inform an actor or director that they are essential to the meaning of the dialog or scene. They are never inserted merely to tell an actor how to deliver the lines; this is both disruptive and unnecessary if your dialog "speaks" for itself, as it should.

An example was given in chapter 1 to illustrate exposition in dialog:

```
                    LAURA
                 (sighing)
         Well . . . it's bound to come out,
         one way or another. Mrs. Rutherfurd
         was here.
```

It was necessary here to explain how Laura speaks these lines since they are open to other interpretations. They could have been spoken briskly or sharply. Instead, she spoke with reluctance and her hesitancy is implicit in the parenthetical instruction.

CAMERA ANGLE DESCRIPTIONS

CLOSE-UP: A shot that emphasizes a detail—a mouth, hands, ball, or signpost.

CLOSE SHOT: Shows a character from the shoulders up and includes some background detail, used often in television. Should not be confused with CLOSE-UP.

MEDIUM SHOT: Shows one or more persons, as in MEDIUM GROUP SHOT. The shot is usually waist high and up. Most directors think in medium shots so it is not necessary to identify them in your script.

LONG SHOT: The next shot after the MEDIUM SHOT. It includes the entire body or bodies and more detail of the scene. It is also used to reveal a wide area or a far distance.

EXTREME LONG SHOT (XLS): Encompasses considerable distance but without definition.

WIDE ANGLE: A variation on the long shot in which a special camera lens is used. It includes more on the sides of the ordinary shot, such as a full shot of an entire semicircular arena.

PAN: The camera is mounted on a pedestal and its head moves from left to right, or right to left. For instance, it PANS an audience, showing many faces but stopping on none.

ZOOM: The camera pulls rapidly forward, enlarging the subject. Example: Camera ZOOMS in on diamond ring.

TILT SHOT: The camera can tilt up or down, giving emphasis to a certain object in the scene. Examples: TILT UP to a figure on a cliff top; TILT DOWN to muddy shoes.

ANGLE ON: Another camera view of a previous shot. Used to emphasize a specific thing in the scene, such as ANGLE ON GIRL looking through fence posts.

REVERSE ANGLE or REVERSE SHOT: An 180-degree opposite shot of the one that preceded it. It alternates between two important subjects, such as two faces in a passionate confrontation.

SPECIAL EFFECTS SHOTS

INSERT: Used to show some detail that is not included in the scene but is important to it. Example: You are describing a battle scene during the Mexican-American War and you want to show a map of the territory over which the fighting is taking place. You write:

INSERT-MAP

of Mexico 1836

The map is not part of the scene that the camera is shooting; it is simply inserted for a moment, then withdrawn. This is not to be confused with a CLOSE-UP of something the camera is already recording. For instance, a man is reading a newspaper and the next shot shows a CLOSE-UP of the story he is reading. That is a CLOSE-UP of something already in the scene, not something which is inserted.

POV (abbreviation of point of view): A cinematic trick used to present a scene so that the audience sees it through the eyes of a particular character. More than that, POV is a means for transmitting the character's emotional response so clearly that the audience must feel the same response. (The character's POV must never be confused with the camera's point of view, which is used more than 98 percent of the time.) Suppose you have a man walking down a hallway. He is carrying flowers, stepping jauntily, and humming merrily. He raps on an apartment door.

You want the audience to react with him to what he sees. It would be written:

```
MAN'S POV

of a masked man holding a revolver.
```

We see the masked man through the eyes of the man with the flowers, and experience the shock he undergoes. (The emotion called for in a POV shot need not be as strong as shock or fear. It can be gentle yet positive, such as sudden recognition, enormous relief, or delight.) POV can also be used to show the point of view of the subject of the shot. For instance, from the POV of a car on a dirt road, it could be written:

```
EXT. - NIGHT - CADILLAC POV

The twin headlights cut through the steadily
thickening fog, revealing a narrow road ahead.
```

We know we are looking into the fog from the view point of the car but not necessarily from the POV of the driver. The viewers are made to feel that they are inside the car, looking out.

REVERSE POV: The POV shot reversed to show the original subject. The REVERSE POV of the example given under the POV definition would be written:

```
REVERSE POV - MASKED MAN

of startled man with flowers.
```

OVER THE SHOULDER SHOT: We see the back of the subject's head from the shoulders up in the foreground while the camera focuses on a specific thing in the background. We know that the object is being seen by the character in the foreground. Example:

```
PARSONS - OVER THE SHOULDER
```

> Favoring Jessica and Audrey as they leave the
> car and slowly walk up the drive, dawdling along
> the way. Jessica looks up, sees Parsons, and
> smiles. He raises a hand in greeting.

We know from this that the viewers will see Parsons's shoulder and the back of his head. We will see what he sees when Jessica smiles. And we will see his hand raised to greet her. ("Favoring" means the person or thing on which the camera is focused in the background.)

SERIES OF SHOTS: Literally a series of shots, run one after another. Used to indicate a passage of time, stream of consciousness, events leading up to a climactic scene, as a marathon race telescoped into 30 seconds and so on. Example: SERIES OF SHOTS—twenty-six-mile marathon race.

SLOW MOTION: The slowing down of the camera. Used to create tension, as in a slow motion shot of a long distance runner as he makes great long strides toward the finish line. Use this shot as a chef uses his strongest spices, with extreme caution.

AERIAL SHOT: Used if necessary to indicate a shot taken from a plane (not a crane) looking down on the scene. These are usually STOCK SHOTS. Example: AERIAL SHOT - PACIFIC OCEAN ATOLLS.

ESTABLISHING SHOT: Compilation of shots which establishes the primary locale of the teleplay. Usually good for the opening of the play. To establish a Western mining town there would be a long shot of the dusty main street with its wooden buildings, hitching rails, and board sidewalks as the camera moves forward to frame Boot Hill at the far end of town.

SPLIT SCREEN SHOT: Used to show two different subjects of the shot on screen simultaneously. For instance, two people are talking to each other on the phone and you want to show the reactions of both.

FREEZE FRAME: The picture stops moving, becomes a still photograph, and holds for a brief period of time.

MONTAGE: A sequence of shots similar to a series of shots. The difference is that more is shown on the screen at the same moment. For instance, two or more different subjects can be blended at the same time like a montage painting. It can be surrealistic or impressionistic. Rarely used in television.

PROCESS SHOT: A shot in which there is filmed action on a screen that provides a background for the subject of the shot. (A character in a car in the foreground, though stationary, *seems* to be moving along with the traffic shown in the filmed action on the screen behind him.) Look for these in most of the police action series.

STOCK SHOT: Films of events previously photographed which are canned and stored in Hollywood. There is stock footage on all recent wars, for instance. Or stock footage on a sailing regatta or a police car speeding through the night (see excerpt from *The Rookies* in chapter 7).

SUPER (abbreviation of superimpose): The superimposition of one thing over another in the same shot. Often TITLES are superimposed over scenes. Or a face can be superimposed over a stream-of-consciousness montage shot. Rarely used.

Transitional Instructions

Transitional instructions—such as DISSOLVE, FADE, CUT TO, and so on—generally are to be avoided unless you know exactly how and when to use them. Even if you feel that they are necessary to stress a particular point, be very circumspect in their use.

CROSS FADE: A specialized editing technique which involves the fading out of one scene and fading in of another. Not to be confused with DISSOLVE since it *always* involves a black or blank screen.

DISSOLVE: Used as a time lapse, not to be confused with cutting from shot to shot. A blending of two shots achieved by the simultaneous fading out of one image (as the screen darkens) and the fading in of another image in reverse density of dark to medium. The first picture disappears into the next picture. This involves the merging of two pictures and never the use of a blank or dark screen. Often used in treatments to indicate the passage of time. (Example: DISSOLVE to the White House.)

CUT TO: The abrupt ending of one scene and the beginning of another—the common transition between scenes. As we have said, writing CUT TO in your script as a rule is redundant since there is no way to shoot the next subject of the shot without cutting to it. Occasionally, however, you might want to employ a tricky cut, in which case it would be specifically designated.

FADE IN: A process in which the picture emerges from a darkened screen to a fully lighted screen. Traditionally, it is used on the big screen to open the film. Because fades are an editing technique, you do not have to be overly concerned with them. However, in television scripts they are commonly used to open and close each act.

FADE OUT: The screen gradually darkens to black, literally fading out the entire picture. Traditionally used on the big screen to end the film. In television scripts all FADE OUTS must end each act which has been FADED IN.

CUTAWAY SHOT: Used to take attention away from the primary action *for a moment*. It can establish a plot point or focus on a subplot facet to give drama or tension to the scene. Use sparingly.

INTER-CUT: The interfacing of two scenes meant to be one scene. Used effectively to show what is happening simultaneously between two subjects. Example: A man and a woman are talking to each other on the telephone. It can be INTER-CUT from the man to the woman, showing their reactions. Or it can be used to INTER-CUT lovemaking scenes between two couples in different locations, though the voices of only one couple are VOICED OVER during the INTER-CUTS.

MATCH CUT: A matching of the subject of a shot in one scene with a similar subject of the next scene. Example: A Christmas tree in a living room. MATCH CUT to a Christmas tree in a department store window.

SUBJECT-IN-MOTION SHOTS

These shots can be handled in two ways: with the camera moving on wheels or with the camera remaining stationary. Both record the considerable movement of the subject of the shot. The rule is: if it is necessary to *accompany* the moving subject in order to see something that enhances the drama of the scene, then designate it as a MOVING SHOT. Conversely, the stationary camera photographs the subject as it is in motion but does not accompany the subject.

Example of a properly designated moving shot:

    PARSONS IN CAR - MOVING

    along a dirt road. It is dawn and the shadows
    make it difficult to see well. He stops at a fork
    in the road trying to decide which route to take.

(The camera is mounted on a truck and moving along with Parsons.)

    FARTHER UP - MOVING

    more slowly as the road narrows. In the b.g. he
    can see what appears to be a string of smoke
    rising from a chimney.

Example of a shot in which *the subject moves but the camera does not:*

    EXT. CADILLAC - LONG SHOT

    The land is barren, dusty. The road winds
    through endless honey-hued hillocks which fade
    into the horizon. The car passes on.

or

    INT. CADILLAC - PARSONS

    rummaging through the lighted glove compartment
    for flask - looks up in time to avoid ramming the
    right side of a cement bridge abutment.

TRAVELING SHOT: A shot in which the camera is mounted on a dolly and moves with the walking subject of the shot. The character must walk a considerable distance (along a beach, for instance) to warrant a traveling shot. If your subject is simply walking from one room to another, it is not necessary to indicate a traveling shot.

DOLLY UP, DOLLY BACK: As it records, the camera moves forward toward a subject or back from it. The same as CAMERA UP or CAMERA BACK.

AUDIO INSTRUCTIONS

Sound is engineered to synchronize with the visual effects on the screen and is as important to the film as any other element. As you begin work on polishing your second draft, search for places in which sound effects will be of special benefit in creating an emotional atmosphere—whether of fright, pleasure, or nervous anticipation. The sound of footsteps dragging down a darkened hallway, for example. You can precede a scene with that sound, an ominous one, which is heard by the viewers but not yet seen.

Sound should always be capitalized in the narrative. (The SCREECHING of brakes, the ROARING of freeway traffic.)

O.S. (abbreviation for OFF SCREEN): The audio instruction used most often. The sound is coming from someone or something OFF SCREEN while the camera is focused on something or someone else. In that shot the actor's dialog is written under his name and in parentheses is written (O.S.) just above his off-screen dialog. Off-screen action which is indicated by sound is written into the narrative. Example: We see two fugitives sneaking through swamp. O.S. the faint BARKING of bloodhounds is heard. The O.S. barking gets LOUDER and LOUDER, as the dogs come INTO VIEW.

VOICE OVER: Written (V.O.), this means that a voice is heard over the action on the screen. Example: We see German troops goose-stepping, children being herded into bomb shelters, soldiers diving into foxholes, while at the same time we HEAR the impassioned speech of a demagogue. This would be a (V.O.)

technique. It can also be used for more prosaic situations. For instance, a letter is being read but we do not see either the letter or the person reading it; instead we see what is happening, in another place and time, which may have a direct bearing on what we hear.

The specific differences are that OFF-SCREEN action (sound or dialog) is temporarily OFF CAMERA, heard only in the background, and could be picked up by the camera if desired; the VOICE OVER source (voice or sound effect) *cannot* be photographed by the camera as the related scenes are being shot.

KEEP IN MIND:

Do not permit your protagonist to be the passive victim of events; he or she must act, not simply be acted upon.

Within the first couple of pages the protagonist must be introduced and made interesting.

Within the first few pages the major problem must be stated.

Each typed page will run approximately 60 seconds on film, whether it is dialog or narrative. Therefore 120 pages = 2 hours of film. (Exception—situation comedies which are double-spaced. See *Phyllis* script, chapter 7.)

Scenes run no longer than 3 or 4 minutes, on an average.

Correctly identify the subject of each shot if you use the shot-by-shot technique.

Write your rough draft with feeling; the subsequent drafts with your intellect.

Have the climax in mind before committing anything to paper.

Allow four to six months to a year for the final draft of an original two-hour teleplay.

Keep the script moving.

Don't direct on paper.

3

How to Write the Teleplay

Television evolved from motion pictures and shares many similarities, both technical and creative, with its parent industry. However, it is necessary here to elaborate on its unique differences.

Unless you are thoroughly acquainted with these differences and know how to incorporate them in your scripts, your fine writing might be unmarketable.

THREE-CAMERA, ONE-CAMERA

Basically, television is shot in the three-camera or one-camera technique. These techniques were developed in the early days of television during which videotape was used instead of film (as in the big screen picture). Because of videotape's limitations, it is used mainly on three-camera shows which are shot on sound stages. However, many shows which are taped are transferred to film.

A three-camera show does not mean that only three cameras are used to shoot the show; nor a one-camera show that only one camera is used. These are simply terms used to designate the two types of shows based on location—inside and outside.

The main thing to remember is: a three-camera show cannot be shot outdoors and utilize moving props. It sticks to its stage set, and all scripts are written around that particular set.

The one-camera technique is used for shows shot outdoors on location, such as *Streets of San Francisco, Family,* and *The Waltons.* There are sets in each, of course, such as Lieutenant Stone's office in *Streets;* but the action moves away from them and out into the hilly streets. So a one-camera show simply means that the highly mobile camera(s) go where the action is and are not confined to the studio sound stage.

The three-camera technique is used for shows shot on the sets, sometimes before an audience. You are familiar with many of these sets—the living rooms in *All in the Family, Maude, Phyllis,* and *Rhoda;* the precinct room in *Barney Miller;* the newsroom in *The Mary Tyler Moore Show.*

You never see Maude, Phyllis, or Mary drive anywhere in an automobile. Rarely do these shows leave the sets in order to be shot on locations specifically built or leased for a particular scene. This would be too costly. In most of these shows, however, one or more additional sets are regularly used. (For instance, in *Phyllis,* there are the commissioner's office and outer office, both located on the same sound stage.)

For an outside or one-camera show, your teleplay can be opened out more than in the three-camera or inside show. Your characters and action can cover a wide territory and you may choose from a variety of locations (as long as it is not set in Timbuktu or some other place which does not have a reasonably believable counterpart in southern California).

As for the inside or three-camera series shows, you must confine the action to the established sets. Occasionally a special set will be built if a scene is so vivid or so hilarious that it is justified. But don't risk it; write your teleplay with as few strikes against it as possible.

Keep the budget in mind. In television, millions of dollars are not invested in a single production as they are in motion pictures. *Streets of San Francisco,* for example, goes on the air every week so that building expensive sets or moving the entire crew to a foreign location would cost a prohibitive sum. But you do have much more latitude where locales and sweep of action are concerned in one-camera shows than in the three-camera or inside shows.

Suppose you are writing a television movie instead of a series script. This will be a one-camera show and must also be written with the budget in mind. For instance, stories focused on sea adventures are almost impossible to shoot because of technical difficulties. So it is wise to avoid them. Don't include any special effects, such as the parting of the Red Sea, that will cause nervous breakdowns in the budgeting department, nor any scenes that require maneuvered crowds of people. If you wanted to write, or rewrite, the Ben Hur saga, you would have to eliminate the great chariot race. Remember that a large number of extras, particularly if they are professionals such as singers, dancers, or circus performers, will be so expensive that your script might be turned down for that one reason alone. If you write a nightclub scene in which there are twenty chorus girls, chances are it will never be produced. With only two or three chorus girls, the story would have a chance.

The size of the home screen is another reason to avoid scenes in which a vast number of extras are involved. They cannot be as effective as they are on the big screen. Television action must come from your characters' inner conflicts or conflicts with each other, not from armies or angry mobs.

CONCEPT, STORY LINE, SYNOPSIS

Ways to present a condensation of your story ideas other than treatments or outlines are: (1) concepts, (2) story lines, and (3) synopses. Novices should never submit these presentations by themselves; you must be willing to write one complete script, if for no other reason than to declare your genuine commitment to teleplay writing.

A *concept* is the theme around which a series or teleplay can be developed but which has not been written. It is approximately 1 typed page or less in length. Concepts can fall into several categories:

situation comedies, serials (daytime or nighttime), episodic dramas *(Columbo, Quincy)*, anthologies *(Police Story)*, comedy-variety shows *(The Sonny and Cher Show)*, children's programs, religious or educational programs. Movies for television can also be condensed in this manner.

Suppose you had the idea for the series which has become *The Quest*. Your concept might begin:

> A Western with psychological overtones in which two young brothers search the Territories in the 1880s for their sister who has been kidnapped by the Indians. Emphasis on realism rather than on Western mythology.

You continue with thumbnail biographies of the brothers (one is city-bred, having been a medical student in San Francisco; the other has been reared by the Cheyenne Indians). Then you touch briefly on the kinds of adventures in which they will become involved (being falsely accused of a sheriff's murder, witnessing the massacre of an Indian village by troops of the U.S. cavalry, etc.).

One of the best and most successful concepts was the one for *Upstairs, Downstairs*. This would begin:

> The exploration of the relationship between two diverse but interdependent groups, the masters and the servants in a wealthy household, set in London during the period before, during, and after World War I.

A *story line* is a slight elaboration of the concept, usually no more than 2 or 3 pages long, in which you present the bare-bones plot for a single teleplay. The problem is stated, the principal characters are named, and the plot should include the major crisis and the climax.

A story line for the *Phyllis* script excerpted in chapter 1 and chapter 7 would begin:

> PHYLLIS is distraught because it is her forty-fifth birthday and no one is eager, or even willing, to come to her birthday party. When her co-worker, HARRIET, says that it must be terrible not to have any friends, Phyllis gets her dander up. To prove that she has the best of all friends, she calls MARY RICHARDS in Minneapolis and asks her to come to San Francisco to see her. She hangs up without explanation so Mary assumes that Phyllis is in deep trouble and needs her.

You go on to explain that Mary does come, is enraged by Phyllis's selfish and childish reasons for summoning her, and calls a halt to their friendship then and there. (A crisis.) Phyllis agrees that she is too self-absorbed and decides to try to be more like Mary, considerate, helpful, and kind. The next day she attempts to put these traits to work in her office and, in her usual bumbling manner, brings Harriet to tears and creates a serious rift between DAN, her boss, and LEONARD, another supervisor. (A second crisis.)

Your resolution of the problem will round out the story line and bring it to the predetermined climax. This can be easily accommodated in 2 pages of typed script.

A *synopsis* is only 1 page or less, in which you disclose the general theme of your already completed teleplay. You would begin a synopsis of *Frankenstein:*

> An European doctor secures corpses from graveyards and dissecting rooms and uses them to construct a 9-foot creature which he brings to life. Too late he realizes he has created a soulless monster.

You then briefly describe the conflicts resulting from the monster's going on a rampage, and their ultimate resolution.

THE DIFFERENT KINDS OF TELEPLAYS

In the previous chapters you learned the essential elements of teleplays and how to use them with some precision in transforming a wealth of jumbled ideas into a cohesive and structured teleplay. You have studied how to write a teleplay; now you want to know what kind of teleplay to write.

It will be helpful for you to have a copy of the *Television Market List,* which includes all the names of the current series and anthologies, their production companies, and the contact for each show. Under the name of the show you will be given the following information: (a) the kind of show it is (situation comedy, episodic drama, etc.), (b) whether it is staff-written, (c) a brief description of its plot format, and (d) whether it requests submissions through agents only.

(You can get the *Market List* by writing to Writers Guild of America, West, Inc., 8955 Beverly Boulevard, Los Angeles, Calif., 90048, $2.00 to nonmembers of the Writers Guild.)

The *Market List* includes episodic comedies (situation comedies), comedy-variety shows, episodic dramas, anthology series, serials, and serializations of novels. In addition to writing for these particular shows, you have other choices: pilots you have conceived for a new series, daytime serials (soap operas), children's programs, religious programs, audience participation shows, movies for television, and documentary and educational programs for public television.

An episodic drama series is one in which each segment (or episode) is a completed story written around continuing characters *(The Waltons, Hawaii Five-O)*. This is also true of episodic comedies *(All in the Family, Laverne and Shirley)*.

An anthology series is one in which a completed story is presented each week, with an entirely new cast of characters (*Police Story,* many of the *Wonderful World of Walt Disney* shows, and *Quinn Martin's Tales of the Unexpected*).

A comedy-variety show usually features a star or stars in a weekly program which specializes in music, dancing, comedy sketches *(Sonny and Cher, Tony Orlando and Dawn)*.

A serial is a series in which the weekly stories are open-ended, without a conclusive climax until the final episode. Think of them as stories "to be continued" *(Rich Man, Poor Man—Book II)*. All soap operas are serials.

A serialization of a novel (mini-series) is just that, another open-ended series which follows the plot of the novel and is brought to a final climax in less than thirteen weeks *(Captains and the Kings, Roots)*.

In the *Market List* you will notice that some programs are listed as (tape), others as (film). This means that originally they were shot on video or film, which indicates to the writer that a taped show is a three-camera show and shot on interior locations; a filmed show is a one-camera show and can include, for instance, car chase scenes.

Write or phone the contact person on The *Television Market List* for the show for which you want to write and ask which script format is used—double-spaced throughout with minimal directions or the standard film form.

A staff-written show means that a staff of writers, directed by the story editor, are assigned to write that show. This does not mean that you cannot submit material to the show's producer through your agent. Fresh new plot ideas are the lifeblood of all television series and a vitalizing transfusion will find a welcome.

Many shows request submissions by agents only. However, if you have an industry contact who can arrange to have your script or treatment read by someone connected with the program, don't hesitate to make your submission through him/her. Use every door that is open to you.

The following pages, taken from the *Television Market List* for the 1976–1977 season (printed by the Writers Guild of America, Inc.), provide you with examples of the information included in the *Market List*.

These lists are updated twice a year.

Marstar Productions Inc.
1901 Avenue of the Stars
Suite 1900
Los Angeles, CA 90067

> ### WESTSIDE MEDICAL
> ABC, 10:00 P.M., Tuesday
> 60-minute episodic drama (film)
>
> The series concerns three young doctors—two men, one woman—who are involved with an up-to-date, modern practice. The personal contacts between the characters are emphasized.
>
> Open for submissions.
>
> Contact: Alan Armer, Producer   466–6491

Mimus Corporation
1313 North Vine Street
Hollywood, CA 90028

FISH

ABC, 8:30 P.M., Saturday
30-minute episodic comedy (tape)

The series concerns the exploits of the character Fish from "Barney Miller," who—facing his impending retirement from the police force—joins his wife Bernice in running a "group home project" for 5–7 year-old delinquent children.

Submissions through Agents only.

Contact: Steve Pritzker, Producer
           Barbara Corday, Story Editor
           Barbara Avedon, Story Editor   663–3311

Paramount Television
A division of Paramount Pictures Corporation
5451 Marathon Street
Hollywood, CA 90038

BUSTING LOOSE

CBS, 8:30 P.M., Monday
30-minute episodic comedy (taped in front of a live audience)

Staff written. All scripts committed for the current season.

Contact: Larry Kasha, Producer   463–0100
                                           (cont.)

(Paramount Television—Cont.)

FUTURE COP

ABC, no air-date set
60-minute episodic drama (film)

This is an action-adventure police series which involves two old-timers teaching a rookie who is an android.

Staff written. All scripts committed for the current season.

MRS. BLANSKY'S BEAUTIES (Miller-Milkis Productions in association with Garry Marshall and PTV)

ABC, 8:00 P.M., Saturday
30-minute episodic comedy (film)

Nancy Walker is a director/choreographer/wardrobe mistress/mother hen to fifteen show-girl dancers at a not-too-prosperous Las Vegas hotel.

Submissions through agents only. All scripts committed for the current season.

Contact: Bruce Johnson, Producer
Marty Nadler, Story Editor   463–0100

QM Productions
1041 North Formosa Avenue
Los Angeles, CA 90046

QUINN MARTIN'S TALES OF THE UNEXPECTED

NBC, 10:00 P.M., Wednesday
60-minute thematic anthology (film)

A suspense-terror thematic anthology.

Submissions through agents only.

Contact: Nina Laemmle, Exec. Story Consultant
851–1234

R & R Associates
c/o William Morris Agency, Inc.
151 El Camino Drive
Beverly Hills, CA 90212

CPO SHARKEY
NBC, 9:00 P.M., Wednesday
30-minute episodic comedy (tape)

An episodic comedy, taped in front of a live audience, that features Don Rickles as a chief petty officer in the navy.

Staff written.

Contact: Aaron Ruben, Executive Producer
           Gene Marcione, Producer   845–7000
                                               (over)

If you have an idea for a series, you should write a treatment, outline, or concept. You can include this with the synopses of twelve additional segments. (Series are presented in blocks of thirteen episodes, which is the length of one television season.) Once some interest is shown in the script by a producer, network, or studio, it would be advisable for you to write a complete teleplay of the two-hour pilot or one of the weekly episodes. Your agent will want to submit this as an indication of your sustained writing ability, your ability to create a total script.

REASONS FOR REJECTION

There are many reasons why teleplays are rejected, in addition to the obvious ones of poor writing, plotting, characterization, dialog, and, of course, the unprofessional presentation of your material.

These reasons will spring from your ignorance of the following principles.

ESTABLISHED LOCATIONS

When you are writing your teleplay, be certain that you know whether it is a one-camera or a three-camera show. The most common reason for the rejection of otherwise acceptable scripts is a writer's inability to make the distinction between these two. Writers who submit a one-camera script for a three-camera series (say, *Phyllis*) and include action which occurs in several locations other than the established sound stage sets are courting a rejection slip.

SERIES CHARACTERS

The second most common reason for the rejection of series scripts is that writers do not fully understand the nature of the characters in the series. Charlotte Brown, co-producer of *Rhoda,* says that they often receive scripts in which the characters simply "do not sound like our characters." Listen to the way the series characters talk, learn their vernacular. Be sure the characters in your script act and react as the continuing characters would. Confine your speculative script to the characters already established rather than introducing new ones (except for very minor characters who have only a few lines of dialog).

DERIVATIVE PLOTS

Another reason for the rejection of scripts is derivative plots. If you were intrigued with a plot written for a specific series in which Phyllis falls in love with a sailing instructor, don't write a script in which she falls in love with a golf instructor.

BUDGET AND TIME LIMITATIONS

Whichever kind of teleplay you choose to write, you must be mindful of two factors that will influence the kind of reception it will receive from potential buyers. These are *budget* and *time.*

You need to be concerned with the budget because television, unlike the big screen movies, simply cannot pour millions of dollars into a single teleplay. Consider that a series will be aired week after week, usually for a minimum of thirteen weeks, and you will see that budget must be a prime factor when a script purchase is being considered.

Study the series for which you intend to write and decide whether it is a one-camera or a three-camera show. If it is a one-camera show in which the action covers considerable territory, you will notice that there are also some established sets. In *Kojak,* for instance, even though the action moves through the streets and alleys of Manhattan, there is also Kojak's office, which has become a familiar set to viewers. In *The Waltons,* which is shot on location, the action roams around the mountainside and into the college town, but the Walton's house and its rooms are used over and over again.

Three-camera shows, either on tape or film, are produced on a sound stage, and it is necessary to be as aware of the established sets as you are of the continuing characters and their personalities. Think of the Bunker's living room in *All in the Family,* the shabby precinct office in *Barney Miller,* Brenda's apartment in *Rhoda.*

When writing for these shows, study the sets and try to keep all action within them. Don't destroy your script's chances by specifying additional sets; these would have to be built or leased at considerable expense.

Another way to keep ahead of budgetary restrictions is by the use of stock or process shots. If you are writing a one-camera show in which you need a train, plane, or ship moving in the distant background, you can be reasonably certain that stock footage (defined in chapter 2) of them is available; indicate them as STOCK SHOTS. A PROCESS SHOT (defined in chapter 2) will show two people in a car that seems to be moving along with the busy traffic seen on the screen behind them. Such process shots eliminate the need to transport the cast and crew at great expense to the actual location. Examples of each from *The Rookies, Blue Christmas* are:

    EXT. STREET–NIGHT (STOCK)

    as our black-and-white cruises by.

and

```
INT. CAR-NIGHT (PROCESS)

We see the lights of the street passing by. Both
Terry and Chris are relaxed, just starting their
shift.
```

As for the time factor, you must learn to structure your script within the 30, 60, 90, or 120 minutes allowed for it. Unlike big screen films, teleplay scripts must be closely tailored to the clock. A 30-minute script plays for 26 minutes and cannot run 1 minute over. In a script written in the screenplay format, 1 typed page equals 1 minute of film. (For exceptions, see chapter 4.) Blanche Hanalis says in her interview (chapter 5) that you must allow some elasticity for the demands of your material. If, for instance, you want the camera to dwell on a particular view, this will consume many extra seconds which may result in a shorter script—but not a shortened film.

It will be very beneficial to study as many teleplay scripts as you can, particularly those for which you want to write. Write to the person whose name is listed as the contact in your *Market List,* stating that you are a writer with ideas for that particular show and would like to have a script so that you can become familiar with its format. Direct the typed letter to the production company address. Keep it brief and professional.

If you do not receive the scripts you request, you might ask your local librarian (or high school or college librarian) to write for them. Librarians will have more clout than you do because they can request materials for general use. If you live in the Los Angeles area, you will want to attend one of the shows that is filmed before an audience.

CENSORSHIP

Few subjects are taboo on television now. Each of the three networks has a Standards and Practices Department which is concerned with the intent of the projects in progress. As Louis Rudolph, ABC executive, says, "If the subject matter is maturely and conscientiously treated, as a rule there are no enforced taboos."

The use of excessive violence, sex, and profanity do come under scrutiny, particularly in programs aired early in the evening before the kiddies are bedded down. Also, scatological words get short shrift. You may use "hell" or "damn," but never the more explicit gutter terms that describe a person's heritage, body functions, or sex habits. The time may come when such language will be acceptable to the home viewers but it is not here yet. Remember that your teleplay will be seen by an extremely heterogeneous audience. What may not perturb a twenty-five-year-old iconoclast could shock a sixty-five-year-old Sunday School teacher—and bewilder a fourteen-year-old Girl Scout. Your responsiveness to the sensitivities of your wide audience and your innate good taste will dictate just how far you can go.

There is one area to which you must be sensitive—the use of ethnic groups or characters. The safest way to avoid offense is by not using characters who are, or seem to be, caricatures of a particular group, such as Mexican-Americans, Indians, Jews, Poles, or blacks. Our society is enriched by this variety of people, as your teleplay will be if they are presented honestly rather than as buffoons or stereotypes.

In the teaser you cannot show an act of violence. You may show a gun being fired and dissolve to a man falling—but the murderer and the victim may not be seen simultaneously.

BELIEVABILITY

Always strive for credibility and never ask your viewers to believe the unbelievable. That is slovenly and, in the end, a negation of your intention—to use the magic of the medium to spellbind your viewers. If anything on the screen makes them say, "Oh, come now. Who could possibly believe that?" the spell is broken. (Exceptions are fantasies or science-fiction teleplays in which the viewers are expected to suspend their incredulity.)

For instance, a girl who has been reared since birth in an Eastern city and schooled in a convent cannot come West, hurl herself upon a half-wild horse, and gallop gaily off across the desert. The viewers are going to wonder when and where she learned to ride like that.

THE ROUGH DRAFT

A rough draft is your first attempt to assemble all those elements on which you have been working, to bring order out of chaos. Now your characters must move into action; now they must speak through your dialog. Open the floodgates of your imagination. Write this draft without revisions or polishing and don't plague yourself about its literary quality. If something does not seem quite right, despite your painstaking planning, leave it and plow right along. Bring your work to the climax you have chosen for it.

Now we advise you to do something that is always difficult. PUT THE SCRIPT AWAY FOR A FEW WEEKS. Don't pick it up again until you feel that you have acquired some degree of objectivity toward it. Its weaknesses and faults will be clearer to you now and you will be better able to rework them for your next draft.

During these fallow weeks you should spend a lot of time watching television with a very critical eye. Note the length of the scenes, the specific subjects of the shots, and changes within each of them. Consider how the scenes flow into each other and how they rise to crises, intensifying to the climax at the end. Note that scenes seldom run longer than 3 minutes, each one representing a change in time or place or action. Note how often the camera is moved and try to identify CLOSE, PAN, MOVING, PROCESS, and so on. Watch out for exposition. Are you aware that you are being told a fact or facts to explain an event? If it is obvious to you, the writer has not been successful with his exposition. Judge how well the dialog explains a character, both by what he says and the way he says it. Take lots of notes in preparation for rewriting the rough draft.

REWRITING

Now you are back at your desk, ready slowly and carefully to write the next draft, or next few drafts, until you have perfected all the elements and believe the script is ready to send to your agent. For the average professional filmwriter each draft takes approximately three or four months. Don't be discouraged if your script, from first to final draft, takes as long as a year.*

Begin to make deletions and additions, to search for the right word, the telling gesture, the imaginative and revealing dialog, dramatic sound effects. Now is the time to be absolutely certain about the subjects of the shots and to have them clearly identified. Write so that the reader will be able to visualize your script with ease. No contractor can understand how a structure is to be built without specific blueprints from the architect; your script is the blueprint for the teleplay.

In order to know the correct format for the construction of this new draft, and how to give it a professional presentation, you will need to refer often to chapter 4, wh re explicit instructions are given on how the dialog and narrative sh ¹ be presented, as well as on necessary camera and transitional dire ns.

Put your dialog to the test: does it revea character, is it true of him/her? Is it exactly the way he/she would speak? Could what it says be better "spoken" through some other human sound—a groan, a giggle?

Ask yourself these questions: Do the action and dialog have balance and rhythm? Is everything—dialog, sound, visuals—indispensable to the delineation and impetus of the plot? Are more of them needed? Are the crises sharp? Is the climax inevitable but not predictable? Is the conflict so strong that the viewer really cares about "what happens next"? Is there enough tension and/or emotion, not only between characters but also in the situations that involve them? In comedy is there enough spontaneity and sense of the ridiculous to make the audience involve itself in the farce?

---

*This pertains to a two-hour pilot; an episode comedy can be completed in two months.

Script Format

As you begin writing your final draft, which may be a third, fourth, or even fifth draft, another important facet of teleplay writing will concern you: How do I make my typed script look professional?

Here again, there are no absolute rules concerning the format in which a script is typed. We intend to give you general guidelines that will ensure a thoroughly professional appearance for your script.

In chapter 7 you will find slightly different presentations in the scripts, but bear in mind that these are not first or fifth drafts, such as you will be writing. They are shooting scripts and are presented here in their actual formats. You will not be writing a shooting script.

Script formats for the various television series differ. Some start with a Teaser and contain two acts. Others, such as the MTM Productions, do not use a Teaser but have two acts and end with a 1-minute Tag. A Teaser is a brief, provocative scene which serves as a lead-in to the teleplay. A Tag is a short scene which comes after the climax and wraps up the teleplay (like the dénouement in a novel).

Do not concern yourself about how to find the correct format for your teleplay. Use the following standard screenplay format for submission to your agent. It is readable and professional. If the show's producer likes your script, he will provide you with a sample script from which to rewrite your teleplay.

Variations of script formats are presented at the end of this chapter.

SCRIPT TITLE PAGE

Drop twenty single spaces from the top of the page and type your title in the center of the page. It must be in caps, bracketed in quotes, and underlined.

Drop another four spaces and type, in caps and lower case: Written by, Teleplay by, Story and Teleplay by, or Screenplay by—whichever you choose. It is centered on the page.

The title page for a teleplay written for a specific series should state the series title in caps. Drop several spaces from the top and type the script title in caps and lower case, underlined and in quotes.

Drop another two single spaces beneath this and type your name in caps and lower case, also centered on the page.

Title pages vary according to the source or origin of your teleplay material. If the teleplay is based on a novel, play, or short story by another author, drop eight spaces beneath your name and type: Based on the novel, "Such and Such." Drop another two spaces and type: by. Drop two more spaces and type the author's name. This same format is used if your script is based on characters from another source. Instead of typing: Based on the novel by, etc., you type: Based on characters from, etc. All lines are written in caps and lower case.

In the lower left corner, about 2 inches from the bottom, type the number of the draft—whether First, Second, or Third Draft (though you will seldom if ever submit your first draft). Single-spaced beneath it, type the date.

In the lower right corner, also about 2 inches from the bottom, type your name, address, and phone number, or those of your agent. These are also single-spaced, in caps and lower case.

In each lower corner, the top lines should be parallel to each other. Example of a title page for an original script:

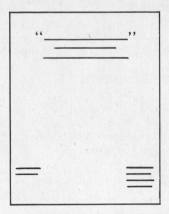

After the title page you can include a page listing the cast breakdown and another listing sets and locations. This, however, is not absolutely necessary for every episodic program, only for those, such as *Rhoda* or *Sanford and Son,* which have established characters and sets. You might want to include exterior and interior set lists for a script written for a show such as *Streets of San Francisco.* Again, it is not required.

The cast names are centered on the page, typed in caps, double-spaced, and written in a column. The word *C A S T* should be written in caps and centered on the page four spaces above the characters' names. (There should be no descriptions of the characters following their names—except for their ages if they are of particular significance.) The sets and locations are handled the same way unless the lists of the exterior and interior scenes are so extensive that they require two columns.

The page would look like this:

SETS AND LOCATIONS

Exteriors
     Metropolitan airport

```
   Busy city street
   Entrance to swank Fifth Avenue apartment building
   Veranda of elegant apartment
   Freeway midnight
Interiors
   Airport cocktail lounge
   Elegant foyer of Fifth Avenue apartment building
   Police lab
   Reception area doctor's office
Stock shots
   "Indianapolis 500"
   Explosion of ships at sea
   Ticker tape parade metropolitan city
   Half-time football game
```

TYPEWRITER SETTINGS

Facilitate your typing by first adjusting your typewriter settings to the seven points which you will use consistently throughout the script. (The top and bottom margins, which cannot be set except in your mind's eye, should be about 1 inch deep each.)

Tab your settings on these numbers:

PICA type: 17   28   35   43   66   72   75
ELITE type: 20   33   42   51   79   87   90

These are used to indicate:

Left margin—17 pica, 20 elite

Dialog—28 pica, 33 elite

Parenthetical directions—35 pica, 42 elite

Character's name (above his dialog)—43 pica, 51 elite

Transitional instructions—66 pica, 79 elite. (Exception: FADE IN is always on *left* margin.)

Page number—72 pica, 87 elite

Right margin—75 pica, 90 elite

The settings for situation comedies are different. The top and bottom margins should be about an inch and a half deep each.

Tab your settings on these numbers:

PICA type   20   29   42   55   60   75
ELITE type: 24   35   50   61   72   90

These are used to indicate:

Left margin—20 pica, 24 elite
Subject of the shot—20 pica, 24 elite
Narrative—20 pica, 24 elite
Parenthetical Direction—29 pica, 35 elite
Dialog—29 pica, 35 elite
Character's name (above dialog)—42 pica, 50 elite
Transitional instructions (except FADE IN)—55 pica, 61 elite
Links of narrative—60 pica, 72 elite
Page number—75 pica, 90 elite

EXAMPLE

SUBJECT OF THE CAMERA SHOT (or scene locale)

Description in narrative form is typed here,
two spaces beneath and single-spaced. SOUND
and camera directions such as ZOOM or INTO VIEW
are in caps. If a CHARACTER EXITS, it is also in
caps. Drop two spaces for the name of the
CHARACTER speaking, written in caps.

                    CHARACTER
          Dialog is placed here, three
          inches in length and single-spaced.

                    SECOND CHARACTER
          (Parenthetical how
          line is spoken or the
          actor's gestures. Also
          includes O.S. and V.O.
          instructions.)
          Dialog is written here, just as above.

And if some action interrupts the
dialog, that action is written into the

narrative until the action is completed
and the script returns to the dialog.

                         SECOND CHARACTER (CONT'D)
            Dialog is resumed after the inter-
            ruption.

                                     DISSOLVE TO:

SUBJECT OF THE SHOT or new master scene

FORMAT RULES

These words should always be typed in caps: ACT ONE, ACT TWO, etc., SCENE LOCALE, SUBJECT OF THE SHOT, EXT. and INT., NIGHT, DAY, CHARACTER'S NAME above the dialog, NEW CHARACTER introduced into the narrative, all SOUNDS, CAMERA DIRECTIONS, and SHOTS.

Spacing rules to be observed:

Single spacing—dialog, narrative, character directions, camera directions, scene descriptions.

Double spacing—between the speeches of different characters, between the subject of the shot and the character's name, between the narrative and the character's name, scene, or subject of the shot or camera shot that follows it.

It is important to break long narrative passages into paragraphs if such passages begin to crowd the page. So, after four or five lines of narrative, double space and continue with it. Let some light in, leave some white space.

If you break the script into acts, type ACT ONE, TWO, THREE, and so on in caps and underscored in the center of the page about 1½ inches from the top. Drop two spaces to FADE IN.

FORMAT FOR TREATMENTS AND OUTLINES

The title pages of treatments and outlines follow the same format as that of the screenplay or teleplay (see above), just as do those of all other forms of submission.

On the first page of the treatment or outline, the title will be centered on the page, about 2½ inches below the top border. It will be typed in caps, underlined, and bracketed in quotes. Drop two spaces and type, in caps and lower case: Written by. Drop another two spaces and type your name in caps and lower case. The date is typed two spaces beneath your name. These of course are all centered on the page. Centered two spaces beneath the title you may want to type: A Treatment for an Original Teleplay, or: An Outline for an Episodic Series. This is not necessary, however. The body of the treatment is typed double-spaced. The names of all characters, when first introduced, are typed in caps. (See excerpt from a treatment of *Kingdom in the Dust* in chapter 7.)

Some treatments/outlines are broken into three acts or more and must be designated as such. ACT ONE is underlined, written in caps, and set apart from the narrative by double spacing. It is written against the left margin.

If you are writing for a specific television program you may begin the outline, preceding ACT ONE, with a Teaser which will contain the opening scene of the teleplay.

Remember that a treatment is 15–45 pages long, an outline is 7–12 pages long. Keep in mind that brevity and dialog are of paramount importance to your presentation.

VARIATIONS FOR TELEVISION FORMATS

Television scripts differ slightly from movie scripts. It would be wise to write to the various shows and request sample scripts, explaining that you are interested in writing a speculative script for them (see chapter 3). Generally, however, you can be safe in following the instructions given for typing screenplay scripts.

Nearly all television scripts begin with a Teaser, followed by two to six acts, depending on the length of the teleplay. The acts are necessitated by breaks for commercials (and are not to be confused with the three-act structure of your teleplay).

Teleplays follow these basic formats:

30-minute teleplay:
  28 to 31 pages; preceded by teaser of 2 or 3 pages
  Acts One and Two, approximately 13 pages each
60-minute teleplay:
  58 to 61 pages; teaser of 3 to 9 pages
  Acts One, Two, Three, and Four, approximately 14 pages each
90-minute teleplay:
  88 to 90 pages; teaser of 4 to 9 pages
  Acts One, Two, Three, Four, Five, and Six, approximately 14 pages each
120-minute teleplay:
  110 to 120 pages; teaser of 4 to 10 pages
  Acts One, Two, Three, Four, Five, and Six, equally divided after teaser

Each act should rise to a suspenseful or poignant moment so the viewers will not be tempted to switch channels during the following station break. These peak points are necessary in comedies as well as in dramas. However, you do not need to be concerned about the commercial breaks because these will be changed many times prior to shooting.

TAPE FORMATS FOR SITUATION COMEDIES

Study the situation comedies. These are half-hour shows and each uses a slightly different script format. There are approximately 26 minutes of actual playing time. Because the scripts are double-spaced throughout, the screenplay rule (1 page = 1 minute of film) does not apply. In the situation comedy format, 1 page = 30 seconds. Therefore, your script will be approximately 45–50 pages long.

Do not worry about this now, however. You will work closely

with the show's story editor after your script has been purchased. (See excerpt from the *Phyllis* script in chapter 7; note the specific script format differences between it and the screenplay format shown in excerpts from *The Rookies*. For example, in *Phyllis* all narrative is in caps and single-spaced, while the rest of the script is double-spaced throughout.)

NUMBER OF SCRIPT COPIES NEEDED

If you do not trust your own typing, have a professional typist make the final presentation copy of your script. If you do this, your instructions must be explicit and leave no room for innovations on his/her part. You will want several copies of your script, so have it copied by Xerox or IBM. You will need to send only one copy to your agent. But after he accepts it, you will have to send along at least six copies. Such duplicating is a real time-saver since it would take years for one script to make the rounds from director to producer to studio heads to actors. This also applies to your teleplay treatments.

"Spec" scripts—those written on speculation without being assigned or commissioned by a producer/director—are the proof of your expertise and must be as clean and readable as possible.

Do not include pictures, maps, sketches, or any extraneous matter. Your script must stand on its own without gimmicks.

FOLDERS

The major agencies have their own presentation folders which they will substitute for yours to make sure that what they submit is easily identifiable. However, bind your scripts in inexpensive three-hole folders fastened with brass cotter pins in order to hold the pages together without risk of having a few slide out and into obscurity. If there is a professional script typing service in your area, their binders are also acceptable. Do not use any other kinds of folders, no matter how much more attractive they seem to you.

5

Interviews

We have tried to put ourselves in your place as we conducted the following interviews with successful and influential members of the television community. Always uppermost in our minds were the questions we thought you would ask, the facts in which you would be most interested, the advice which you would find most useful. Each interviewee was very responsive to this approach and his/her answers consistently were directed to you, the novice teleplay writer.

All interviews were taped, then edited with the cooperation of the interviewee, to provide succinctly the information we believe you will find most helpful.

BLANCHE HANALIS
Screenwriter

Mrs. Hanalis was born in Ohio, raised in Chicago and New York, and is now a resident of California. She is married and the mother of three.

Her writing credits include more than 250 produced television and feature films, among them: *The Littlest Leaguer, Weddings and Babies, Kitty Foyle, The Rose Bush, Dear Charlie, Family Affair, The Lieutenant, Courtship of Eddie's Father, The Bold Ones, The Further Adventures of Oliver and the Artful Dodger, The Trouble with Angels, Where Angels Go, A Tree Grows in Brooklyn, Little House on the Prairie, A Home of Our Own, Young Pioneers, One and Two,* and *The Hideaways.*

In television, the writer must establish the premise, the characters, build towards a climax and resolve the story within the half-hour, hour, 90 minutes, or two hours allotted. The audience must be captured quickly, which calls for a technique somewhat different from that in feature films where there is a captive audience who have paid to get in and are going to remain to find out what is going to happen. In television the audience can quickly flip the dial and often does. If they're not held in the first few moments they may be lost no matter how good the piece is after that.

There should be no difference in the quality of writing whether it be for television or feature films for the large screen. I, for one, get just as excited about the things I write for television as I do about the films I do for the large screen . . . perhaps more so. I'm often overwhelmed by the thought that what I have written is reaching an audience of forty or fifty million people in a single night.

I'm not sure "writing" can be taught, and I've been reluctant to teach although the opportunity has been offered me. One CAN be taught the mechanical or technical aspects of television and filmwriting, however, which is quite another thing. The prospective television and filmwriter should watch as many films as possible; should read as many scripts as possible; should try to become familiar with format and how the camera is used. It's important to understand the camera, especially in television, because it's a tool for "grabbing" an audience immediately.

Much depends on the nature of the material. In a "police show," for example, opening on a piece of action called "the tease" is usually effective . . . and it is a tease intended to hook the audience immediately.

Since I have no particular interest in "police shows," and since the things I do are usually character oriented, my television pieces build more slowly, with the characters, hopefully, serving as the hook. An example: The two-hour script I wrote for *Little House on the Prairie.* The story began with a break with old ties, the old home, the departure, going into the unknown . . . and the audience, which cared about the people, remained to see what the future held for them.

A picture I wrote for Bell Telephone last season, *A Home of Our Own,* was based on the true story of a Catholic priest who built a home for the lost and discarded children of Mexico. Since the story covered a time span of twenty years, and I was going back and forth in time, I found it helpful to use narrative, or "voice over." The narration was always over "action," and since the story was being told from the priest's point of view, it was always his voice that was heard, helping the audience understand three years or perhaps, five years, had passed. However, since television is a visual medium, I feel narration or voice over should only be used when necessary or if its use contributes to the literary quality.

In *Young Pioneers* I began with the marriage of my protagonists because I felt an audience would get involved immediately with my sixteen-year-old bride and her eighteen-year-old husband. The picture opened on Molly's diary. (In that period many women kept diaries.) We heard Molly's voice reading from the diary: "On this day I become David Beaton's wife, etc." We then dissolved into the marriage ceremony, and the first "line" spoken was Molly's "I do." In this instance the diary and narration were natural vehicles . . . and I continued to use the diary and Molly's voice over all through the picture.

In television, as well as for the big screen, the writer is often given a book to adapt. The one luxury in writing for the big screen is time. The deadline is reasonably flexible. The script is required in two, three, perhaps six months. In television the script must be written, cast, shot, cut, scored, and be on the air in the precise time slot previously scheduled. The television writer usually works under the gun.

Writers are usually asked what alchemy turned them into writers. I'm afraid I can't answer that. It seems to me I always knew I was going to be a writer; that it was what I had to do. I doubt if my beginnings were unusual. I edited my school paper and reviewed books for a Chicago newspaper, not only because I loved writing reviews but because it was a way to get books I couldn't afford to buy. When the youngest of my three children started school I knew the time had come to apply myself fully to what I had always wanted to do . . . write drama. Because I had spent so much time indoors in front of the television set with my children when they had the usual childhood ailments, I felt comfortable with the medium. I'm afraid I'm too impatient to attempt a novel. I love seeing my work performed; I love seeing it come to life.

I began by writing a script. Since I had no idea about any special technique I wrote my story in play form. I did, later on, take a course at Queens College, one night a week, to learn about format and camera . . . but it did come later, and it was helpful. The instructor was associated with CBS and took the class to the studio to see a show in rehearsal. Television wasn't filmed at that time and my first show was also live. I wrote a one-hour script titled *The Littlest Leaguer* and someone suggested I send it to the William Morris Agency. I'm afraid I didn't have the faintest idea what a William Morris was. At any rate, the Agency signed me as a client, sold the script almost immediately, and it went on the air within six or eight weeks.

It was a prime-time show sponsored by Alcoa-Goodyear and in retrospect I can't imagine how I got that lucky. Since it was my first effort I was paid whatever the minimum was at that time, $3,000 or $3,500. I'm happy to announce I'm paid considerably more now for my work.

I was fortunate in that there was a marvelous cast in *The Littlest Leaguer,* it was beautifully directed, and the show was warmly received by the critics. (The *New York Times* called it the best comedy of the season.) The show was nominated for an award and I'm afraid I was so naïve I thought there was nothing terribly unusual about this.

I then participated in a film called *Weddings and Babies* that won a Silver Lion at the Venice Film Festival, which only enhanced my naïveté. I was delighted, though, when I was asked to write *Kitty Foyle,* to be aired live five days a week. It was an exciting experience for a relative novice, with the producer pulling the pages out of my typewriter as fast as I finished them. If a writer can survive that he can survive anything. I left the show, or I should say, the show left the air after six or eight months, but I've never regretted having done it. I learned I could write under pressure and it's stood me in good stead.

Shortly after that, Columbia brought me to Hollywood to do *The Trouble with Angels,* which starred Rosalind Russell and Hayley Mills, and the sequel to it, *Where Angels Go.* Other writing assignments followed.

Not all my scripts have been filmed, of course. For instance, one of my scripts which was supposed to be a major feature film and which was already cast, the director hired, was canceled abruptly because of budget problems. This kind of thing can and does happen.

If I could give any advice to writers who are just starting out, I'd tell them not to worry about the technical aspects of filmmaking. The only thing that really matters is the characters, the story, and telling that story in the best possible way. New writers have a tendency to get overwhelmed by technique and technical problems. Neither is terribly important as compared to creating real people; nothing is as important as the drama. If the audience gets involved with the characters and the story, all else can be resolved.

Novice writers should know that before they're established they're rarely consulted about script changes. While this does not happen to me any more, in the beginning I had things go on the air I didn't recognize as my work. In fact, I've had some experiences in which the entire point of view was changed. There isn't much a writer can do about it except resolve not to work for those people again . . . and hope to never be so poor or hungry you have to.

Most writers have their own "modus operandi." For example, I don't do treatments because I find that by the time I've written the treatment I'm through with the project. I've said what I wanted to say and I want to move on to something else. The networks and most producers now accept this as one of my "peculiarities." On rare occasions I run into one who won't and who insists on a treatment. We part company, hopefully still friends.

I imagine there are other writers who follow a like procedure. I think through my story then make a rough step-outline on a yellow pad, listing, usually in a line or two, the master scenes. It's really a blueprint that doesn't make much sense to anyone but me. I write pages about the characters for my own benefit, things which may never appear in the script but which I want to know; things which will help me understand my people as though I've known them all my life. This is a "luxury" of course unless one is involved in a major project. On the other hand, it's not necessary when one is writing for a half-hour series in which the characters have already been well established such as in *All in the Family.* Anybody capable of writing comedy should have no problem understanding those characters. They are beautifully limned and executed every week.

I am a visual writer. I am the camera . . . and if the camera is used as it should be there will be times when no dialog is necessary. A writer should write a scene as the camera's eye will see it, and use the camera fully. In *Young Pioneers* I felt it was important for the camera to be on a tight shot of our young couple's clasped hands during the marriage ceremony. I felt it was important to visualize the reaching and holding; hands locked together. Young hands.

I simplify my shots and camera directions but make a point for the camera when I think it's important. When I called for a *long shot* or *extreme long shot* out on the prairie it was because I wanted the director to know I was looking for a sense of the vastness of the prairie; the isolation. It's the director's prerogative to agree or disagree. The writer can only hope the director will agree.

If I feel a speech or reaction is important, even vital, my camera direction simply reads: ON MOLLY. If I feel the camera should be close on two characters, I indicate it. If there is "action" behind or in front of my characters, I indicate it, and the camera direction may read: ON MOLLY . . . CAVALRY IN F.G. (or b.g.). The director may see it differently and shoot it differently; may decide to do a close shot of the character and then pan swiftly to, say, the cavalry. But I do believe the writer should indicate how he SEES the scene.

I work with the director only when we are preparing the shooting script so that I can make whatever structural changes he wants or feels he wants to make the picture work visually for him. Actually, the producer is only entitled to two drafts and one polish of a script, but I feel it's to the writer's advantage to stay close to the picture as long as possible . . . and when possible. I like to see the dailies and voice my opinion but it's a sad fact that once the script is finished, producers and directors like the writer to get lost, disappear forever, forever meaning until they need the writer for another project.

I really can't explain HOW I write other than that I do my blueprint of the master scenes and get to know my characters. I then write a fast first draft, frantically fast, perhaps because until I write FADE IN and FADE OUT I don't believe it's going to "happen." I scramble through that first rough draft, and it *is* rough, but at the end I have a pretty good idea whether or not I'm going to have a picture. I then take a deep breath and really get down to work, starting at the beginning and going straight through again. What is supposed to be a first draft is actually not a first draft at all, but I find this is the only way I can work, so I do.

It's important that a writer consider location problems. There's nothing to be gained by writing what's impossible to shoot, although there's not terribly much that isn't possible with our technology and when you have the best special effects people in the business as we do in Hollywood.

In the *Young Pioneers* Christmas special we were faced with a problem. How does one shoot a Christmas show in August, in Arizona? It's not possible to snow-in a whole prairie. Ergo, I decided to open with a flashback. We opened on a sound stage which could be snowed in. The camera moved through the snow to the interior of the sod house and held on a diary. We HEARD the entry in the diary narrated by our protagonist: "December twenty-five, eighteen seventy-four: I shall always cherish this Christmas since we have shared it with dear friends and good neighbors, etc." When the narration reached: "It is difficult to realize that only a few short months ago, etc." we dissolved into the prairie . . . and it was summer. Our story unfolded, building to the point where preparations were being made for Christmas . . . and we were once again on the snow-covered sound stage. It was effective . . . but more important, it worked.

Before a picture goes into production I go through the script with the director, hoping we'll be of one mind. It doesn't always happen. Although I try to write my scripts to time out properly, it's not always possible and I much prefer to cut the script than have the finished picture mutilated because it runs too long. A script should be orchestrated and if the woodwinds are suddenly pulled out it's not going to be much of a symphony.

In feature films it doesn't matter if a picture runs a little longer than anticipated. In television it's not only a disaster, it's impossible.

Based on my own experience, 90 pages is approximately the right length for a two-hour show. However, it does depend on the subject matter. In a show where, say, one wants to take advantage of the visual beauty of the setting, or where the setting tells part of the story, time must be allowed for the camera to do its work. In an "action" show, more can be told with less.

I don't time my acts, but I do try to anticipate what will make a good act ending. I think most writers have a second sense about this, and while I try to think through act endings I don't let it inhibit me. It's hard enough to accept the fact that your story is going to be interrupted by commercials. One can only hope the commercial won't break the mood of a scene one has nurtured lovingly. It's not a bad idea, however, to leave a problem suspended at a possible act end. The cliff-hanger has always been and will always be a marvelous device.

In a half-hour show it helps to find the middle break. The script runs approximately 35 pages and the commercial will come in at page 17 or 18. It helps to gear the script towards this point.

Writing is an endeavor in which one is judged only by what is on paper. Once there is access, once one has a foot in the door, everything else depends on the words. Although minimum fees for a writer's services have been set by the Writers Guild, a writer who is in demand can negotiate the monies to be paid. There is a so-called ceiling, but the writer who is in demand, and who has a good agent, can make a superior "deal."

Contracts take forever to prepare, but a deal memo is drawn up immediately which spells out the major points; what the piece is, what monies are to be paid, or percentages, if possible, and the start and finish dates. The memo is only the bones of the deal, but it's important to have it before one word is put on paper.

I'm a compulsive writer, I'm afraid, and I work seven days a week except for brief holidays. I love writing. I know there are some writers who don't, and it must be terribly painful for them. I'm a night worker, starting my "day" at 2:00 or 3:00 A.M. I usually work until noon and schedule my meetings in the afternoons.

If I'm going to presume to advise new writers, I'll have to start with a cliché. Write. Don't be discouraged. Each script you write, each time you rewrite it, and rewrite it, you are getting closer to perfecting your craft. Most new writers are impatient. Having written a script, they feel it is ready to be filmed. The truth is, and not only for new writers: the first thing one writes isn't IT. It is only the germ or skeleton of IT. Now comes the thinking and rethinking; the time to let it evolve; a time to find the flaws; to find the weaknesses. I doubt there's a single writer of any stature who hasn't written and rewritten and rewritten; thought and rethought . . . until what is finally seen by the audience is the product of a long and often painful process.

Many times while I watch my work on the screen I'm filled with second thoughts, misgivings. I should have done it differently. It would have been better another way. It really never ends. I'm never completely satisfied and often dissatisfied. I'll probably always feel this way. Perhaps it's just as well. It's not the grasping but the reaching that matters.

AARON SPELLING
Producer—Writer—Director

A native of Dallas, Texas, Mr. Spelling attended Southern Methodist University and the Sorbonne. While at SMU he was the first playwright since Eugene O'Neill to receive the Harvard Award twice for the best original one-act play. He directed plays at the Playhouse, the Margo Jones Theater, and the Dallas Little Theater. In 1953 Mr. Spelling came to Hollywood and acted in more than fifty television shows and a dozen movies.

His first writing assignment was with Dick Powell's *Zane Grey Theater;* during one season he wrote ten of the twenty-nine segments. He branched out into all phases of television writing, including a script, *The Last Man,* for Playhouse 90. Later he wrote the screenplay for 20th Century Fox. He created the *Johnny Ringo* series and produced it. He became producer of the *Zane Grey Theater* and other shows, and was executive producer of *The Smothers Brothers Show.*

In partnership with Danny Thomas (Thomas/Spelling) he produced *The Danny Thomas Hour, The Guns of Will Sonnett, The Mod Squad,* and six Movies of the Week.

Mr. Spelling formed a partnership with Leonard Goldberg in 1969 and since then the Spelling-Goldberg Productions have produced thirty motion pictures for TV. Their ABC series successes include *The Rookies, S.W.A.T., Starsky & Hutch,* and *Family.*

He has been involved in the production of sixty television movies and has been honored by such diverse groups as the Television Academy, the Writers Guild of America, the Hollywood Foreign Press Association, the Producers Guild, and various nationwide social and medical organizations, as well as receiving five Image Awards from the NAACP—more than any other film industry producer.

There are three producers: the executive producer, the producer, and the associate producer. I don't know that there is too much difference between the executive producer and the producer except in certain series and certain movies. In independent companies the executive producer is the owner of the company and functions as a buffer between the producer and the network. For example, it would be the executive producer who creates an idea or buys an idea from a writer. His first job as executive producer would be to take it to the network and sell it as a development deal. This means that the network will give him the money to bring in his writer and get a script on the property. Then his job is to sell the network on shooting the pilot or the potential series. Once that pilot is given the green light, then it is usual to bring in a producer to function as the on-the-line producer of the project. That producer would then hire an associate producer.

Let's see if I can tell you what the guidelines are for a property, once it goes into production. The producer, with the executive producer, does the casting and hires the director. Then the producer, not the executive producer, would go with the production manager to scout locations, attend all wardrobe meetings, attend all production meetings that would deal with the props that are necessary for the production, and the staffing of the crew, etc. The associate producer, in turn, functions as his right-hand man; functions mostly in the post-production area. In other words, after the pilot is completed, it's the associate producer who then does the dubbing and scoring of the film. All films have three producers. In our company, as an independent, sometimes an executive producer or I, as executive producer, might function as the producer of the property but usually we have three. Sometimes there is a cross-over. We occasionally produce our own pilots and movies and we take only producer credit, not executive producer credit. But if we hire a producer then we take executive producer and the producer takes producer credit.

Executive producers have a very close working relationship with the producers. We still see dailies, which are films shot every day, with our producers. A producer can handle the casting but we have all the approvals of casting. The producer's basic concern for a movie for television (there is a difference in a series) is to be with the company at all times. He is on location. The movie we are shooting now, for example, has nine days of location. We are the executive producers, and we also have a producer. Obviously we can't run our company and be on location with the picture, so the producer does that. He reports to us on casting, we see dailies, and we are in on the editing of the picture with him.

Networks never act as producers, nor should they be allowed to.

Their job is basically over once they give you the commitment. This is not a democracy, no theater is democracy. And if you let too many people have a say-so you come out with a hodge-podge. It has to be the style of one person or, at most, two persons. Once the network gives you the commitment they can see the film and they might ask for a change or a cut—a standards of practices cut, sometimes called a censorship cut. But they do not produce the picture.

A producer never puts up his own money for a pilot. The gamble is just too great. What happens is that the network, if they want to go ahead with the project, gives you a certain amount of money to make that pilot. If you go over that, then that is your problem.

We could go on for two hours about what a producer does in television. It's so much more far-reaching than in motion pictures. Motion pictures, whether we producers like it or not, is a director's medium. It is by far a director's medium: it is a director's last choice of casting, his last choice of script, his last choice of editing. Not so in television; it is strictly a producer's medium.

The producer in television is an enigma. It's a whole new ball game. The first question the network asks when you give them an idea for a new series is or if you sell a pilot, "Who's going to produce it?" They don't care who's going to star in it or who's going to direct it or who's going to write it. They think that if you get a good producer it is his job to bring in those other talented people. I think the biggest stars in television today are the producers.

We will often finish a movie or a segment of a series, and the director is already off directing something else. He doesn't even figure in the post-production. He doesn't even do the editing of the film. All he has is just the first shot at editing in television. He gets to see it the first time, he makes his changes and then he is through. I wish I could say that all of my directors hang around and supervise the editing and post-production music but they don't.

It's a financial problem for them, really. You don't make the money directing television that you do in a feature film. A good director can do one feature a year and make $250,000. In a television movie where our top is $20,000, or a television segment where our top is $6,500, the director has to direct an awful lot of television in order to make a living.

Let's consider the basic ground rules between the producer and the network. There is a set price for a television movie, for example. That price usually ranges, depending on union increases, from $650,000 to $750,000, for a movie for television. This is given to the producer by the network.

I'll give you an example of the film we are shooting now, *Come Little Ladies of the Night.* We read a *New York Times* article and loved it. We went to the network and told them that this will make a very good two-hour movie for television. They agreed with us. Step 1: They gave us the money to buy the article. So it was their risk, not ours. This is the way it is done all the time. Step 2: They gave us the money to hire a writer to see whether the subject matter could work in a script form. Still their gamble, not ours. For example, they may have paid, in this particular instance, $7,500 for the article and $20,000 for the writer. So we now have $27,500 invested. We now get our script. If the network at that point says, "We don't like the script, we've changed our mind," you shake hands and bid each other a fond adieu and that's it. But you've had no risk except your time. The network has risked $27,500. That's as it should be because, since the networks have the final say as to whether the script goes to picture or not, an independent or a major producer would go broke developing projects for a network at his own expense if the network keeps turning them down. If you do ten of those you've suddenly lost $275,000.

The networks have what they call their own development fund and they give you the money for the story and for the script. If a network says, "We like the script. Let's go to film," then we are given a set fee to do that movie. In this case I think it was $700,000. Now it is our gamble and our risk. For that $700,000, for which the network gets two runs, we have to make the film and pay the residuals on the second run. If we are good producers and it comes in at $700,000 we have broken even, but we have gotten our fee which we have put in the budget, as producers and executive producers, and we also own that film in perpetuity—it's ours—not the network. We can sell it to foreign syndication. And that is your profit. If you're lucky and everything functions right, you may make that film for $650,000. You don't have to give the $50,000 back to the network. That's your profit. That's what we try to do but it all depends on what the subject matter is and how much you love it. We did one project for which we got $650,000 and it cost us $950,-000. We try to make it up on future movies. And that's the way it functions. If that movie costs you $850,000, you better have a good foreign sell or you're going to be in trouble.

You can multiply that by twenty-two in a series. For example, we have an idea for a pilot and the network tells us to develop it. They give us the money to write the script. They like your script and give you the money to shoot the pilot. Usually it's X amount of dollars for an hour's pilot, about $400,000. If you make it for less than $400,000 you are in good shape. If you spend more, and invariably you do, then it comes from your pocket.

It's a calculated gamble you're taking. Let's say you go $20,000 over in your pilot. It's worth it to get the best you can on the screen because then you have a chance of selling a series. Once you sell that series the network gives you a price per episode—you negotiate that out. Usually that ranges between $200,000 and $300,000 per episode. However, producing a good pilot is no guarantee that the network will buy it. It's the biggest gamble of all. Only one out of every six pilots sells. I think that at ABC alone this year ninety pilots were made and only nine or eleven were bought. It can be a ratio of 10 to 1. Each network makes a multitude of pilots that are never sold. That's as it should be. If you did it on a 1 to 1 ratio, that means that no matter what you make, they are going to put it on the air.

We hear a lot about packaging, but that is a very abused word. If an agency offers a package, you assume that they are bringing you an idea, a writer, a director, and a star and that they sell it for you. That is the meaning of a complete package. Unfortunately, it doesn't happen that way. As a company you sign with an agent first; you don't handle it on a deal-to-deal basis, you don't handle a package at a time. For example, let's assume that our company were to sign a deal with one of the big agencies as a packager. Well, that agency

may bring us a package; they very well might not. Let's assume that
a writer walks in my office and tells me an idea which I like. We go
ahead with the script, with the network's approval, and we cast it
and it's sold. That agency with whom we're signed still gets the same
10 percent as if they had brought us the idea and the writer and the
director and the producer.

We don't have an agency now and I doubt that we ever will again.
Take an average television show that sells for a series of $250,000
an episode and the agency gets 10 percent. That means $25,000 that
you are not seeing on the screen. It's almost impossible to make that
much per episode. If an agency takes $25,000 an episode and you
do twenty a year, that's a half a million dollars that goes to the
agency. It's almost impossible to ever recoup unless you have a
runaway hit. And don't forget that the agency gets 10 percent of all
foreign sales.

The best way for a writer to sell a pilot or a television movie is
to have his agent submit it to producers, as such. Just submit it and
no packaging. *No packaging.* Just tell his agent to submit it as a sell.
No matter how good it is, I wouldn't even read it if it were submitted
as a package.

An agency should be satisfied to make 10 percent of what the
writer gets. That's the reason agencies were formed. This whole
packaging syndrome is on the way out. It is only used now in variety
shows and some comedies. I don't know of many dramatic shows
that have a packaging fee now.

There are two ways in which we get most of our scripts. Seventy
percent of the time, we will read something in a newspaper or book
or magazine or we will work out an idea with our story development
people. Then we bring in the writer and the writer will develop it
and write it. The other 30 percent or 29⅞ percent of the time,
writers will meet with our movie development people and present an
idea which we will take to the network.

My big anger about writers is that the new writers, the young
writers, come in and complain because they can't get started in the
business. If I ask to read some of their work, they say, "What do you
mean?" They don't have any or they'll write you a 1-page outline

or they'll submit a story. There is a scarcity of writers. We look every day for them and I think we use more new writers than anybody. If new writers want to write for a *particular series,* they should sit down and write a script for it and submit it through an agent. But don't come to us with it. You can't do that when you're a writer and a member of the Writers Guild. We're not allowed to ask writers to write spec scripts and we wouldn't want to. But how can you really know if the writer can write unless he writes? He's not an actor, he can't come in and read a scene for you.

My advice to young writers, any new writers, it's very simple: you watch TV, and you watch and you watch and you watch, and you say, "Gee, I can write for that show." Then write that company and say, "I'm a beginning writer and I would like to have a copy of one of your scripts just to get the form." We will be more than willing to send a copy of the script. Then he writes his script and sends it to the story department through an agent. What a pleasure to get to read a script free! We buy it if it's good. Automatically that writer has to join the Writers Guild, but he's a writer and he has a credit.

Sometimes an agent calls and tells me there's a young writer who's terrific and asks if I want to meet him. I say, "No, I would not like to meet him." I don't care whether he's seventy or ten years old, or whether he's fat or thin, or whether he's blond or brunette. What good is it going to do to meet him? Is he going to talk a good script for me? I think you're often misled by that. My answer is that I would love to read something he has written. You'd be surprised how many times the answer is, "Well, there is nothing you would really like to read." Then he's not a writer.

Sometimes we will meet young writers and read something of theirs and let them at least write a story. If it's good, we'll go on to the screenplay; if not, we'll say to them, "Hey, we gave you a shot but you're not ready yet." At least you have a story credit and you can get in the Guild. Then we move on to another writer.

Novice writers now have something else—there are so many movies for television being made, you can write a movie script on spec. It's not like you're writing for a series and if it doesn't sell to that show, you're dead. Movie scripts are invaluable things. You can write them and if they don't sell to movies, you can try to sell them to movies for television. A complete film script should be two hours long. That gives you the opportunity to sell them to movies or television. I would say between 105 to 125 pages.

An interesting thing is happening now in films. The tail is wagging the dog. We used to do small pictures on television which the movies said weren't big enough for movies. But now they will do the small picture and television is seeking a bigger concept. That small movie that we used to do for television when we were doing 90-minute movies, we are no longer allowed to do. It is unfortunate, for there were some brilliant pieces of work that came out on that. I don't think this is temporary. I think it's gone to the two-hour picture. The network thinks that they need bigger concepts.

In our organization we have a reader whose job it is not to turn anything down. The reader will read a project submission and then give us 3 or 4 pages on it. If we like it then the reader will send us the whole property. In too many companies the reader's job is to reject what she does not like. We don't have that. Our reader's job is to read and synopsize everything for us.

I think that your idea of advising writers to submit a synopsis with their scripts is terrific. But it should be presented only with the script, never alone. I think writers can synopsize their material better than any reader. It's a tremendous shortcut and I think every producer and every reader would appreciate that. I think all agents should do it, too. It would be a great idea if agents were smart enough to synopsize or if they got the writers themselves to do it.

I would tell writers that, right now, the climate of our times being what it is, 70 percent of the movie scripts being bought are hard action for male stars. That's for motion pictures. But in television we won't do caper pictures. That's a no sell for us. You can't get the networks to buy one. Television audiences just don't like them. Television audiences like the unusual. The network will ask us for a two-sentence or one-sentence concept. And if the concept is exciting, that's a sell. That's a very important thing for writers to understand—concept. We are doing *The Boy in the Plastic Bubble,* which is definitely a television concept. It's about a kid who is susceptible to all kinds of germs and has to live in a plastic bubble the rest of his life. It would never be made into a movie.

If writers want to write for women stars they should write for television. There are very big box-office stars in television. We know if we can get Elizabeth Montgomery for a movie we are going to get a big rating. If you can get Marlo Thomas to do a television movie you're going to get a big rating. Angie Dickinson would be a big rating. So we have developed women stars in television. I can't explain it but while motion pictures have not been developing female stars, we have in television.

It's unbelievable to me, though, that Barbara Stanwyck and Joan Crawford and Bette Davis aren't working. These great actresses who want to work aren't working and it's the fault of the networks—they are full of bull, they are crazy, they are nuts. I've done three movies with Barbara Stanwyck. All three of those movies average over a 40 share. I haven't even gotten the network to agree on a concept for her in the last three years.

When we're searching for a writer, sometimes we will ask agents for suggestions. But most of the time we pick the writers we know or have read something by. I would say that happens 60 percent of the time. The other 40 percent we'll want writer A or B who will not be available so we'll have our story department call the agencies and they submit some writers' names and we choose one of those. So that's where an agent can help a writer.

The only way that I know for a writer to become established as a Movie of the Week writer, or a television writer, is to write scripts on spec and submit them. Once he sells one, then he is in demand. I think we use more new writers than anybody, but I don't remember our ever hiring an unknown writer to write a movie, in all the sixty TV movies I have produced. Except once. It was a strange experience. A producer who used to work with us brought a new young writer in on a film. The writer came in and did a first draft and it wasn't bad. He did a second draft, and it wasn't bad. But eventually the producer had to do most of the polishing himself. The young writer said, "It really wasn't my cup of tea but I do thank you for getting me in the Guild and everything." Then he went home and wrote a script on his own on spec. It was called *Oklahoma Crude* and he sold it for $350,000. His name is Mark Norman.

That shows you that if you have a screenplay to write you should write it. A screenplay can be submitted to every studio, to every star, and then if you don't get a sale there, it can be submitted for television to all three networks. So there is no wasted time writing a 105–125-page script. But you should not waste your time writing something that deals with the poetic development and love affair of a butterfly and a bee because that's not going to sell. And I think writers should just take the time to read a handbook such as yours to find out what the marketplace is, what are they looking for.

TONY FORD
Literary Agent

Mr. Ford was an agent at The Music Corporation of America, 1949–1953. He spent several years as an independent producer and produced many specials for Timex featuring such stars as Victor Borge, Jerry Lewis, Paul Anka and Darren. He also produced several of the CBS Ringling Brothers specials.

Mr. Ford was head of the Television Literary and Package Development at General Artists Corporation, 1962–1966.

In 1966 he opened his own management firm, Tony Ford Management, Inc. This firm was acquired by the William Morris Agency, Inc. in 1968, where Mr. Ford has served as a vice president and head of the Package Development Department since. He was transferred from the New York to the Beverly Hills office of William Morris Agency in 1975.

Agents have very personalized and involved relationships with their clients. I could guess that once every three months it brings me to the edge of what I think is going to be a nervous breakdown; I am that involved with the writers.

You know, there are agents who submit and play the odds. They work on the theory: send out enough stuff and you may sell one. But I become involved. I become involved because I enjoy it. I get great satisfaction and gratification from it. And also the fun of being an adult and being well paid as an expert to play "Let's pretend." That's a great kick. In using the expression "Let's pretend," I don't mean to denigrate the art of agentry.

Most agents work closely with sponsors. There are advertisers like IBM, Hallmark, and Bell Telephone, who are always looking for important dramas. The networks the last couple of years have gotten into what they call the docu-drama—the Sam Sheppard murder case, the Lindbergh kidnapping case. In keeping contact with the buyers, I am what we refer to as a developer of creative services. It is my job to listen to whatever ideas writers have and to stimulate them to create ideas which hopefully will become series. I'm also very much involved with the television movie. Most writers who come up with an idea and are going it totally on their own without consulting a good agent who knows the marketplace are asking for problems. The agent works on two levels—he not only works with the client but he is also in the marketplace, being a sponge and absorbing what the marketplace is saying. This way he can encourage his client to create properties for the marketplace's area of vulnerability.

Many writers sit at their typewriters and decide that they are going to create the great series or the great television movie, and they are working without any conceivable notion of what the marketplace is looking for or what will work.

There are occasions where I will initiate the idea and give it to the writer. I worked with a marvelous writer, Alan Sloane, on the Hallmark production of *Teacher, Teacher*. I knew that Hallmark was looking for contemporary dramas that had to do with issues of the day. The condition of the mentally retarded was and is very much an issue. I asked Alan if he thought a drama concerning a retarded child might interest him. He thought it was a marvelous idea and called Hallmark about it. They were intrigued and *Teacher, Teacher* was created. It won an Emmy Award for that year.

I was very proud when a client of mine, George Lefferts, the writer, a few years ago went up to receive his Emmy and said on the air, "You know I've gotten three of these and I wouldn't have gotten any of them if it hadn't been for Tony Ford." That was pretty damn nice.

I also act as a catalyst between three ingredients—the writer's idea, the actor, and the director. There was a program called *To All My Friends* about the sickle-cell anemia that strikes black people. Bill Cosby, Alan Sloane, and I got together on it and conceived the basic idea. Then I went to Gilbert Cates, who directed *I Never Sang for My Father,* and we literally put the unit together. CBS financed it and it won an Emmy for that year. Again, it was a great feeling.

I'm eager to take new writers . . . eager, eager, eager. I encourage those who are in my department to read everything from new writers, even a writer without a single solitary credit. That is absolutely vital to the medium. (Some writers become so successful they no longer want to work in television because the big thing is motion pictures or the theater or novels.) You also need a constant refreshening of writing styles and abilities so the industry can get new attitudes. There has been a change of Values from the fifties and sixties to the seventies.

I know of one writer, Michael Loman, who came out here without a single credit. He had speculated on a script which did not sell because it was similar to another story that was already being done. But he showed the capability for dialog and plot that energized me and I began to work with him. Suddenly he became one of the most sought-after young writers in the business. In a period of six months he had more episodes than he could handle. He is now generating a series that he is developing with us for NBC. I believe this credit should be shared with the young agent trainee under my supervision who brought him to my attention, Paul Neller.

Yes, we are eager for young writers. It's tough to go through mounds of material but we are most interested in new writing talent. What we try to do is talk to them and evaluate their level of sensitivity, their feeling for characters, their inventiveness, and if you get any vibes at all then you want to sign them to a contract.

A new writer should send a résumé and a synopsis of his current work when seeking an agent, even before sending a script. Sometimes even in the letter itself you can get an idea of the writer's ability, and how well he sells himself. Agents care about a potentially lucrative client, and any input the writer can give on a synopsis to indicate this and stimulate the agent should, of course, be included.

My advice to an aspiring television writer is to *write.* Speculate. If he has an idea that he feels is original and he has not reached a level of acceptance where he has sold anything yet, he should speculate on screenplays or, if he chooses to go into the television comedy field, he should speculate and write a complete episode for one of the hit comedy shows. This can help him improve his craft and will supply him and the agent with a complete sample of his work—plot, characterization, and dialog.

Major reputable agencies do have departments constantly reading new material in hopes of finding the new Abby Mann or Norman

Lear. It should also be pointed out that, prior to submitting to a reputable agent, the writer must obtain the agency's release form, sign it, and accompany it with his submission. I'm sure you will realize the necessity for this when you consider the volume of material submitted to agents.

New writers often suffer from an obvious lack of research and/or sloppy and unprofessional manuscripts, but what puts me off most is *attitude*. This does not mean I expect a young writer to come into my office with a subservient approach or one of awe, but I've had some cocky characters walk in and attempt to convince me that I'm an idiot if I don't buy every word they say or write, as opposed to being willing to exchange ideas. I have had experience with this type and, in most cases, you never hear of them again. Of course, there have been one or two who have gone on to great success by sticking to their guns, but usually the best procedure is to *listen* half the time.

If an agent is worth a damn he will work with a writer on an idea and advise him about its potentials in the marketplace, its strengths and weaknesses. That's the first step in packaging. The second step is to work with the writer in bringing together the other ingredients that will cause the marketplace to react favorably above and beyond the original material. In selling the show *To All My Friends* to CBS, we had Gilbert Cates, Alan Sloane, and Bill Cosby, a strong team of three people who wanted to do the same thing. But each one alone would have a problem.

Usually if a writer comes in with the idea, he is going to do the pilot script. And if he's an important, good, busy writer, he'll write the pilot and then walk away from it. However, he doesn't have to write the pilot. If the idea is that strong and the network reacts well to it, then I advise them that this writer won't do the pilot and ask if they would consider it if we could get a quality writer involved. If they agree, then we try to find a writer to do it. At the same time we must negotiate for the writer who brought in the idea to get a royalty, depending on his stature in the business. He might even get a piece of the profits or royalties each time it runs, but that is a simple matter of negotiation.

New writers, even those with good potentials, often make mistakes. They have the tendency to create their characters as they see them and feel them, where they need to learn to project themselves into the audience's mind, to get a feel of what the audience's common denominator is, so that they develop characters that audiences relate to in today's market. Audiences relate to Archie Bunker. He looks real, he's a guy who lives in a two-family house in Queens and works on a loading dock. Mary Tyler Moore is another character audiences really relate to.

There is a tendency for a writer to get over-inventive sometimes and create either characters or canvases that are foreign to the audience. Writers must develop characters and canvases that the audience is comfortable with and subliminally familiar with, even though they haven't experienced that very same situation. Even in these days of women's lib, a lady truck driver is, at this time, not relatable to the common denominator audience. No one knows what next year will bring because tastes change, values change.

Take lady private eyes. They've tried it out in a few pilots. I must have read twenty treatments. Audiences do not accept the lady private eye and they are uncomfortable with it because they are programmed to see a private eye as Humphrey Bogart or Cannon. He can have unusual characteristics but he has to be a guy. Even people at the networks—program development people who are very much women's lib oriented—know that a lady private eye won't make it today. I don't know what a year from now will bring.

As for merchandising a writer package at my level of agentry, we creatively develop the package and go to the networks with it. And we have another level at the agency where the master negotiators handle the business affairs. They go in and protect the writer package because the writer invariably winds up a partner with a package company. Here is another very important part of packaging: the writer will come in with the idea and if we went to the network with it the network would never buy the package from the writer because the writer is not capable of assuming financial responsibility. The network may say, "We love it, we want to buy it, and we'll give you $130,000 for a half-hour episode." This means that the writer has to deliver those shows at that figure. If something happens and it costs $140,000, he's going to be on the hook, and the network will not accept someone who does not have that kind of money to lose.

The writer has to be protected. First of all, networks know that production companies or corporate entities have the financial where-withal to deliver. So when we negotiate the deal with the network we are usually negotiating for the writer/client and the package company, assuming we're representing the package, and we then build in all the protections. For instance, suppose Chico dolls are made. The production company gets so much per doll and of that percentage the writer gets X percentage. You negotiate all these things in order to protect the writer in every area of merchandising.

I advise writers to include a 1- or 2-page synopsis with their scripts, because you can determine from this whether the canvas and the characters are something you can sell, whether the marketplace is looking for it, or whether it is too far out and not relatable to the audience.

As far as format is concerned, there is a relatively traditional form to a script. A half-hour show can go 30-some pages but it doesn't disturb me if someone submits a half-hour script as a possible series idea and it's 50 pages long. I'll just tell him it's far too long and try to help him with the editing aspects of it and try to give him the basic ground rules.

Usually a team of writers will be developed on a series because they know the characters and can come up with stories that work for them. Maybe six to eight writers—either individuals or teams—will be used over and over because they work out for that particular series. The staff job, as such, on these shows is the story editor, who usually comes from the ranks of the writers who have delivered good scripts. He oversees the material as it comes in from the writers, and he will meet with them to discuss any changes he believes would be beneficial to the script.

The producer hires an editor because the producer is pretty busy, but there are times when the producer works very closely with the editor. Once a producer finds an editor he trusts, he lets the editor take charge of the scripts. Story editors have to establish qualifications for the job and basically they have to have proven themselves as episode writers first.

STUART CHRISTENFELD
Attorney-at-Law

Mr. Christenfeld is a graduate of UCLA, 1966 and a graduate of UCLA School of Law, 1969. He has been associated with the Beverly Hills law firm of Kaplan, Livingston, Goodwin, Berkowitz and Selvin for seven years. For the past four years he has been a partner in the firm, specializing in entertainment law.

You asked about significant clauses which writers should be aware of when negotiating a contract. I will give you an outline of a writer's contract which will illustrate most of the variations and important typical clauses that are included in agreements between production companies and their creative employee personnel. The best example of a writer's contract which includes most of the possible variations is the pilot writer's contract. Typically, the writer is employed by the producer to write a pilot script for a possible series. The agreement will provide the form of work which the writer must write; for example, a story (which is an outline of the sequence of events in a teleplay) and/or a full-blown teleplay itself. The contract will specify delivery dates by which the writer must submit to the production company the various elements of the work. Each delivery is followed by a reading period, during which the production company reviews the material that has been submitted and has an opportunity to consult with the writer so that, if the next stage is reached, the writer will be able to revise or amend the work in conformity with the producer's instructions. For example, the pilot writer's contract might call for a story and teleplay. The story must be delivered by a specified date. This will be followed by a reading period during which the producer and the writer will consult, revise the story, and include the revised story as the basis for a first-draft teleplay, which will then be reviewed by the producer in conjunction with the writer and polished into a final-draft teleplay.

The writer's contract, of course, will provide a schedule of compensation. The compensation can be categorized as follows: first there would be a specified basic compensation for writing the literary elements—the story and/or the teleplay. The amount for this typically ranges from $10,000 to a high of as much as $25,000 or $35,000 for a half-hour prime-time network situation comedy. Most pilot scripts are written for an amount that is somewhere in between these two extremes. Payment of the basic compensation allows the producer one original television broadcast of the pilot. Additional amounts are negotiated for reruns of the pilot. Some writing agreements provide for a bonus if the pilot is actually produced, whether or not the series is produced. Some writers' contracts provide for a bonus if the pilot is produced and a series is sold based on the pilot. These bonuses range in the neighborhood of $1,000 to $5,000.

If the series is produced, the pilot writer will get a royalty for each new episode of the series that is produced and broadcast. The amount is usually negotiated up front in the writer's agreement and the amount will usually depend on the nature of the credit which the writer receives in connection with the pilot. If the writer receives sole credit in connection with the pilot, he may be able to demand an extremely high royalty for each episode of the series. The typical range is anywhere from $500 per episode, which is low, to a high of $2,000 per episode. If the writer receives shared credit in connection with the pilot episode, his royalty with respect to series episodes may be reducible by the royalty which is payable to the second pilot writer. Sometimes a floor is negotiated so that this reduction cannot diminish the pilot writer's royalty below a certain established figure. I want to clarify that these royalties are payable for each new episode of the series quite apart from the question of whether the pilot writer writes that episode. The whole point is that the writer of the pilot episode, by reason of his original creative efforts, is entitled to benefits that flow from the series being produced and broadcast. Even if he never picks up his pen again, he will receive royalties for shows written by other writers because, the theory goes, they are based on characters and situations that were originated by him in his pilot script.

The typical writer's agreement will contain a so-called "pay-or-play" provision. The "pay-or-play" provision is a shorthand description of a contract clause which provides that the producer has no obligation to actually use the services of the writer or to use the results and proceeds of the writer's services (that is, his script), or to exploit or exercise any right which the producer has, such as the right to produce and broadcast a program based on the script or to otherwise dispose of any of the rights which the producer has acquired from the writer. So long as the producer pays the basic compensation and the writer is ready, willing, and able to deliver the literary materials and hasn't breached his agreement and isn't disabled, the producer need never use the script. The reason for the pay-or-play clause is as follows: in certain professions, especially the creative professions such as acting and writing, exposure to the public and the exercise of one's craft is recognized by the law as being an impliedly bargained-for ingredient of the employment and unless the contract between the employer and the employee specifically negates the obligation to exploit the results and proceeds of the creative employee's services, there can be an action for damages brought against the employer by the employee for the employer's failure to produce and exhibit the work. All well-drafted writers' contracts will contain the pay-or-play clause to preclude any possibility that the writer may sue the employer/producer for failing to exploit the work.

The typical writer's agreement also contains certain warranties. The writer is typically required to warrant that the material which is created by him is original, does not infringe on the copyright of any third party, and will not defame, invade the privacy of, or otherwise violate the rights of third parties. The writer is usually requested to indemnify the producer against any damages which arise out of the writer's breach of these warranties. The lawyer for the writer may attempt to restrict the warranties in a variety of ways. First, he may wish to limit the warranty which states that the work will not defame or invade the privacy of third parties to situations where the writer knows or should reasonably have known that his work would be defamatory or would invade the privacy of a third party—as opposed to making the absolute undertaking that these violations will not occur. Second, the writer may seek to put a monetary ceiling on the amount of indemnity that he may be required to pay the producer. If the clause merely provides for a blanket indemnification against damages, there is no upper limit, and if the producer is sued successfully by a third party, the producer would then sue the writer to be reimbursed for the amount that the producer has had to pay by reason of the writer's breach. The writer's attorney may, depending upon the writer's leverage, be successful in requesting that the writer, under no circumstances, be required to indemnify the production company in an amount greater than the production company has paid the writer. For example, if the total amount paid to the writer under the agreement were $25,000, the writer's indemnification obligation for breach of warranty would be up to but not exceeding $25,000, even in the event of a knowing breach by the writer.

The typical writer's agreement also involves a "grant of rights" clause, in which the writer acknowledges that an employer-employee relationship exists between him and the production company pursuant to which the writer grants all rights of every kind in the work that he is writing, including the right to exploit the work in all media including, without limitation, television.

A good attorney will ensure that the writer's agreement includes provisions which trigger the payment of additional amounts of compensation to the writer (over and above the basic compensation that the writer gets for writing the pilot script) if the producer uses the writer's work in various media outside of television in which the producer has the right to exploit it. For example, the pilot writer's agreement may provide that if a motion picture is based on the pilot script, an additional sum of money will be paid to the pilot writer on commencement of principal photography of that motion picture, even though he is not the writer of the screenplay. Again, the theory is that the writer's basic material is being used and consequently he should be compensated. Note that the agreement typically grants *all* rights to the producer, the theory being that the producer has to be maximally free to exploit the work that is being written for him. This is fair so long as the writer is paid each time the work is exploited in the various media in which the producer has the right to exploit it. Furthermore, the Writers Guild Basic Agreement provides certain protections to the writer if the work is exploited in other media. Minimum payments are required even if the agreement between the production company and the writer doesn't contain specifically negotiated amounts. However, the Guild Agreement provides for payments which are typically much lower than those which would be negotiated.

Under the Writers Guild Basic Agreement, the writer may obtain additional payments for additional uses of the material that he has written pursuant to the so-called "separation of rights" clause of the Guild Agreement. The "separation of rights" clause is complicated but, simplified to its basics, it means: if the writer has written wholly original material, either a story or a story and teleplay, not based on material supplied by the producer or assigned by the producer, the writer retains certain rights which cannot be taken away from him, even if he contracts to give them away in his agreement with the producer. (This is because, so long as the writer is a member of the Writers Guild and the producer is a signatory to the Writers Guild Basic Agreement, the Guild Agreement including the separation of rights clause will control over any conflicting provisions in the private contract between the writer and the production company.) No matter what the private contract says, the Guild Agreement says that if the foregoing prerequisites are met, the writer is entitled to separation of rights and, consequently, retains certain rights in his work; these include radio rights, theatrical motion picture rights, dramatic stage rights, publication rights, merchandising rights, and live television rights, unless these are separately bargained for and paid for by the producer.

The typical writer's agreement may well contain a so-called morals clause pursuant to which if the writer engages in behavior which brings him or the production company or the network or the sponsors of the program into disrepute or subjects them to ridicule, certain sanctions are available against the writer. The most typical sanction is the right to delete the writer's credit.

Last, almost every writer's contract will contain a clause which provides the form of credit to be accorded the writer. The credit clause will, of course, be subject to the Writers Guild Basic Agreement provisions regarding credits. However, the writer may be able to negotiate terms that are better than Guild minimums. Especially in the case of writers with substantial negotiating leverage, there will be up-front negotiation and specific inclusion in the pilot writer's agreement of the form of credit that will be accorded the writer in the event that his work is produced as a pilot, and in the further event that the pilot is picked up for a series. For example, if the work is the original idea of the writer and is not assigned to him by the producer, the writer may negotiate for a so-called "created by" credit, which is in addition to his "written by" credit. The contract may provide that this "created by" credit will appear on a separate card and may further provide that the card will appear in the opening credits immediately prior to the producer's credit. There may be a specification of the size and style of type to guarantee that the "created by" credit is no smaller than that accorded to the producer or the director. The "created by" credit is one that typically appears on series episodes as opposed to pilot episodes, in addition to the credit accorded to the writer of the particular episode. The "created by" credit usually identifies the writer or other creator who is responsible for the original idea, usually embodied in the pilot script that led to the series. An example is the "created by" credit that Norman Lear receives on all episodes of *Maude*.

The model that I've just described is a writer's employment contract under which the writer is engaged to write material specifically for the production company. There are alternate methods whereby written material can be acquired by a production company. For example, if a writer has already completed a teleplay, it can be purchased by the production company. The purchase contract will be a literary acquisition agreement, in which the production company acquires the right to exploit the already written teleplay in television and various other media. Basically the same terms will be included, or are included, in employment agreements, i.e., warranties, grant of rights, credit, compensation for use in various media. The purchase can be made by way of option. One can option a teleplay just as one can option a screenplay. For example, the production company could agree to pay the writer-seller $5,000 for the exclusive option to a teleplay that he has already written. Then the producer could attempt to interest a network in the project. However, that is not commonly done in the case of a series. The usual method is to have a pilot script written pursuant to a direct employment agreement between the producer and the writer.

You ask what permissions or releases, if any, a writer would need if he uses a specific newspaper story or magazine article, based on a current true event, as the plot of his teleplay. An example is *Dog Day Afternoon,** which was based on a true event reported in a national magazine and several newspapers. That really involves us in a discussion of questions such as defamation, invasion of privacy, and copyright infringement.

Let me give in broad strokes the kinds of considerations that the production company would weigh in determining whether it would want to acquire a piece of material like this. The production company wants to make sure that it is protected in the use of literary material that is submitted by writers. So any agreement that it enters into with the writer will contain clauses guaranteed to protect the production company, usually in the form of warranties and undertakings by the writer that he has the rights in the material that he is transferring, that the material is original (except to the extent that it is in the public domain), and that it doesn't infringe the copyright of any third party or defame or invade the privacy of any third party. In the example of *Dog Day Afternoon,* it is possible that the production company would require consents from the individuals who are depicted in the story that was based on a newspaper account. To the extent that the writer's story which is based on the newspaper account incorporates protectible portions of the reporter's story—such as the reporter's arrangement of events or the specific language used by the reporter—the production company would require the consent of the reporter or the newspaper, whoever held the copyright in the story.

*About a New York bank robbery.

Practical Business Advice

As you begin to labor in the television vineyards you realize that writing a script, even a brilliant one, is not enough. You want to sell what you have written. You want it screened and seen. Here is where confusion sets in for most beginning writers, and questions arise: How do I market my scripts? What and where are the markets? What are the minimum rates I can expect? What residuals can I get from my script, if any? What do I do about contracts, options, and copyrights? What is the Writers Guild of America and how will it serve me?

Let's begin with the answer to the first question:

HOW TO MARKET YOUR WRITING TALENT AND HOW TO GET AN AGENT

There are very few television producers who will read gratuitous scripts; already their offices are flooded with agent-submitted scripts. So in order to have your script even considered, it must be submitted to producers, networks, or studios (the buyers) through an agent.

Choose an agent, or several, from the list given at the end of this chapter, preferably an agent with a Beverly Hills or Los Angeles address since they are on the scene, are in closer touch with the markets, and can expedite sales negotiations for you.

Next, send the agent a letter which includes all the facts about yourself and your works that will be of interest to him. Include a description of your works, those that are completed, those in progress, or both. Make this brief but not sketchy. Let him know exactly what you are working on and what you have ready to be shown— the more the better. Include with the letter a completed script with a 1- or 2-page story line, outline, treatment, or a carefully written concept for a series or a movie for television, or all four. (See chapters 2 and 3 for details on how these are written.)

If you have written a script with a particular actor/actress in mind, don't hesitate to mention this. Or, having learned through years of television viewing which kinds of shows a particular production company produces, you might suggest where you think your script(s) could find the most favorable reception. Whatever you think will help sell your script, don't hesitate to suggest.

It is acceptable practice to make multiple submissions, so send copies of your letter and your scripts to as many agents as you like. Don't fold the scripts; mail them flat in a manila envelope with a cardboard inserted against the back of the script. Mail a sampling of your works, perhaps a half-hour script, an hour script, a treatment, and a concept for a series or movie. Don't send a great bulky package because agents are inundated with scripts and simply will not have time to wade through so much material. Make your sampling selective.

A good guide for this is to ask yourself: If I were an agent, what would I look for in a prospective client? Would I be more interested in a single script, a one-shot deal, or in a selection of scripts which proves that the writer has an abundance of creative ideas and can be expected to sustain them through a variety of assignments? It is the latter, of course, for which an agent searches. A one-shot script will demand almost as much time and effort on his part as selling a series pilot or concept, or selling you as a writer for a series, which may be remunerative for a long time to come.

Agents are salespeople who need products to sell, so when they look at a new writer's work, they look to the future. They look beyond your particular submission; they evaluate the potentials apparent in the writing and the presentation of ideas. Your scripts must show the agent not only how well you write but the variety and wealth of your creative imagination. Your agent wants to know if you can be a productive client for him, if you have the ability to become the kind of professional who consistently can tap the goldmine of television writing.

Don't start haunting your mailbox immediately or sit by the phone, your hand on the receiver. Agents have dozens of scripts from clients and potential clients on their desks. They can read only so many at night and on weekends. But if your synopses or concepts intrigue the agent, he will leaf through the scripts and form a tentative opinion of them. If he likes what he scans, he will give them a thorough reading. Then you will get a letter or a call from him. Otherwise, your portfolio will be returned—in the stamped self-addressed envelope which you always provide. If this happens, don't despair. There are all those other agents and no single agent's judgment is infallible, as they are the first to acknowledge.

Before you send scripts to agents it is advisable to register them with the Writers Guild of America, West, 9038 Melrose Avenue, Los Angeles, Calif. 90069 (see Manuscript Registration Service in the Writers Guild section of this chapter). They will register completed teleplays, treatments, and series or movie concepts. This registration establishes your claim of ownership of the material and the date of its completion.

You can become a member of the Writers Guild only after you have sold a script or a story line or have had thirteen weeks employment as a television writer. Within thirty days after you have received such a "credit," you will have to make application to join the Guild. This is mandatory, not something you may choose to do only if you want to.

In his interview in chapter 5, Aaron Spelling, a highly successful independent producer, says, "There is a scarcity of writers. We look every day for them." Louis Rudolph, ABC executive, says, "There are a number of good directors and producers but when it gets to good writers, there simply aren't enough." Tony Ford, agent, says that agencies are constantly needing new material "in hopes of finding the new Abby Mann or Norman Lear."

So take heart.

Also, take a train, plane, or bus to Beverly Hills, California, if you possibly can, and visit as many agents as you can. Deliver your scripts to them and be prepared to sell yourself as a serious writer. An exchange of ideas will be to your advantage, but remember that agents have more ideas to exchange than you do. They are professionals who know the television industry inside out and upside down. So listen to them and stifle any belief you have that your genius transcends the marketplace.

It would be a phenomenon if your agent (now that you have one) could sell the first script(s) he submits for you. But he may accept your script—and later, a producer may buy it—on the basis of the talent you have brought to it and on their belief in your ability to rework it into something filmable.

An agent is not only the salesperson for your product. He is much much more. Any good agent is qualified to serve both as your adviser and your critic. He knows what kinds of teleplays are being bought, what kinds are being sought. He knows which production companies are strong in that particular season, and therefore have the greatest need for scripts. Agents are often called by producers and by story editors who need writers to work on certain projects. This gives agents opportunities to recommend new writers. Many agents also work closely with sponsors—IBM, Hallmark, Bell Telephone, etc. —and sometimes, as Tony Ford does, will even conceive an idea which the sponsor likes and will give it to one of his writers to turn into a script. Your agent can also guide you through the intricacies of all business deals; he can save you from costly misjudgments where both your career and your income are concerned. A close relationship with him will be as invaluable to you, almost, as your talent.

If your script appeals to your agent but is not acceptable to a producer as it is, the agent will advise you about necessary revisions or about scrapping it altogether and writing a new script which is more closely tailored to the market. Listen to him; you are paying for his expertise.

Don't hesitate to call on your agent for advice. He is working for you; you are not working for him. If you make money he makes money. But know this, any good agent is worth every cent of his 10 percent.

If your agent accepts a *Phyllis* script but cannot sell it to that program, all is not lost. It remains an excellent example of how you handle comedy, one which he can show to various producers along with other scripts. He is not trying merely to sell scripts or a single script, he is trying to sell you, your talent, your ongoing output. The more diverse your scripts are, the better your chances are at becoming a marketable writer. Also, if you write a two-hour teleplay and it doesn't find a market, it may sell as a big screen movie.

You may have heard that you should submit to networks, with your scripts, a release form (a standard form which they supply and which you sign in order to protect the buyer from any plagiarism suits), but we don't advise this for the simple reason that no *network* is going to read your script unless it comes through a reputable agent.

As for an agent's release form, Tony Ford says, "Prior to submitting to a reputable agent, the writer must obtain the agency's release form, sign it, and accompany it with his submission." These forms can be obtained by writing the agency (see list in this chapter).

Other than through an agent, how can you get your script in the door of a producer?

For one thing, there are your personal contacts. Do you know anyone in the industry, an editor, a staff writer, a director, a friend of a star or a producer, a bit player, a script reader? When you get to Beverly Hills, circulate as much as possible and put yourself in the paths of persons connected with the industry. If they believe in you and your work, ask for their help. Get your scripts in that door any way you can, as long as your integrity and seriousness of purpose are not forfeited.

If you are familiar with the styles of various television directors and feel that one of them is more compatible with your work than others, call the Directors Guild of America, Inc. (213–656–1220) and ask for the name, address, and phone number of his agent. If they have it they will be glad to give it to you. Send his agent your script with a covering letter asking that it be given to the director, and enclose an outline or synopsis of it, plus a self-addressed stamped envelope.

The same applies to the Screen Actors Guild (213–876–3030) if you think there is a role in your teleplay that will appeal to a certain actor/actress. Send your script, covering letter, outline, and self-addressed stamped envelope to the agent. He might get the script to his client.

Your analytical television viewing will have shown you which producers present the kinds of shows for which you believe your talents are best suited. You will find the names of the independent producers in the Writers Guild section of this chapter. If you are not a professional writer as defined by the Writers Guild, send to him the same speculative material you sent to the actor's or director's agents. Make certain that the outline you send is as powerful and provocative as you can make it.

Do not send anything to the television networks except through your agent. It will not be read because of the danger of plagiarism suits and, too, they are flooded with scripts and story lines from independent producers, studios, agents, and publishers. (The exception is ABC, which has its own production company, ABC Circle Films, and your script would go to it, not to the network.)

Television consumes scripts like paper in a raging fire. The possibilities open to writers are almost limitless. Study the programs on television; find out which appeal to you and which seem to be markets for your unique talents. Write to those shows (after you have acquired a *Television Market List*—chapter 3), stating that you are a writer with ideas for their show(s) and would like to have a sample script in order to learn their format.

The various kinds of shows include:

30-minute situation comedies, which occupy the largest percentage of prime time *(Phyllis, Barney Miller)*

30-minute daytime serials *(Days of Our Lives, All My Children)*

60-minute episodic dramas *(Police Woman, Six Million Dollar Man)*

60-minute episodic anthologies *(Police Story, Wonderful World of Disney)*

60-minute serials *(Upstairs, Downstairs)*

60-minute serializations of novels, mini-series, limited series *(Captains and the Kings, Rich Man, Poor Man, Roots)*

60-minute variety specials (showcases for stars such as Neil Diamond, Bob Hope, Johnny Cash, with emphasis on music, comedy, dancing)

90-minute episodic dramas (*Quincy, Columbo*—NBC Mystery Theater)

Dramatic specials *(Eleanor and Franklin, The Lindbergh Kidnapping, Amelia Earhart)*

There are so many choices that you are certain to find your creative niche among them. There are also audience participation shows (quiz shows), children's programs *(Sesame Street)*, educational and religious programs.

"SPEC" SCRIPTS

Louis Rudolph, ABC executive, says: "If we read a script that shows talent, we may not buy that particular script because that concept may not be right . . . but the minute one shows talent, we're going to jump on that writer. We're going to drag him in here."

That's the very best reason we can give you for the constant submission of "spec" (written on speculation) scripts. There is a crying need for writing talent in television and there is no other way to convince producers of that talent except through your scripts. You may "talk" a good story. You may even talk one that your agent or a producer is interested in; but eventually they have to see it on paper. So write your heart out.

Your "spec" scripts may not be bought but your potential as a writer may be. Occasionally, if you are not a member of the Writers Guild, a producer may ask that you rewrite a script or, on the strength of its merits, submit others. Or you may be assigned to work on other scripts, a not unlikely possibility in television. You might then be employed as a staff writer, eventually to work your way up to the coveted position of story editor.

Charlotte Brown, co-producer of the *Rhoda* show, prefers "spec" scripts because they show her that a writer not only understands the continuing characters in the series but can write good situations and dialog. Perhaps she will not produce your script but if the writing intrigues her she might "buy" you as a writer instead.

Agents do not always recognize this and fail to offer "spec" scripts to established shows. Producers and story editors thus never see them. So your agent may need a bit of prodding in this area.

COPYRIGHTS AND CONTRACTS

If you want to copyright your script, write to the United States Copyright Office, Washington, D.C. 20599. Ask for Form D, *Application for Registration of a Claim to Copyright in a Dramatic or Dramatico-musical Composition*. Enclose a check or money order for $6.00. Return the signed form with your complete script. A treatment, outline, or synopsis cannot be copyrighted. Many television writers do not copyright their scripts because once the script is sold to a producer, the copyright becomes the property of the purchaser. However, you may want to do so because, until the script is actually bought, your legal ownership will be secure. Incidentally, don't write the copyright number on the cover of your script.

An accepted procedure is simply to send the script by registered mail to yourself. Keep it (unopened) with the registration receipt in a safe place until it is needed, if ever.

Under the Writers Guild section in this chapter you will find a copy of the *Standard Form Freelance Television Writer's Employment Contract* (p. 133). It explains the areas of negotiation and what you should be aware of when working out the details of a sale.

Your agent will handle all details concerning contracts or options for you. Or you may want to secure the services of an attorney who is familiar with the economic intricacies of the entertainment industry.

Remember that the best way to protect the ownership of your script is by registering it with the Writers Guild of America, West, Inc.

WRITERS GUILD OF AMERICA, WEST

Consider the Writers Guild as one of your best friends. More than 4,300 writers belong to the Guild, of which approximately 2,500 are television writers. As a guild (or union) it negotiates collective bargaining agreements for its membership and offers to its members group insurance, a pension plan, and a credit union; it also serves as a collection agency for writers' residuals (royalty payments for reruns).

There is a vast amount of material published by the Writers Guild, for members only, which is extremely helpful to writers. Because of space limitations, it is impossible to reproduce it here but we have selected the material which is most important to novice television writers. The offices of the Writers Guild of America, West, Inc., are located at 9038 Melrose Avenue, Los Angeles, Calif. 90069 (Phone: 213–550–1000). *All mail should be sent to:* 8955 Beverly Boulevard, Los Angeles, Calif. 90048. It is affiliated with the Writers Guild of America, East, Inc., 22 W. 48th Street, New York, N.Y. 10036 (Phone: 212–575–5060).

A person is eligible for membership in the Writers Guild by obtaining employment as a writer or selling unpublished and unproduced literary material in the motion picture, television, or radio industry. The employer or the purchaser need not be a signatory in order for such a person to qualify for membership in the Guild, but no member of the Guild may render writing services for or sell literary material to a nonsignatory. A producer is not allowed, according to Writers Guild rules, to ask you to write a "spec" script without compensation. However, you may submit "spec" scripts to producers as long as you are not a member of the Writers Guild.

FORM FROM THE WRITERS GUILD
MEMBERSHIP DEPARTMENT

The Guild represents writers primarily for the purpose of collective bargaining in the motion picture, television, and radio industries.

☐ We do not obtain employment for writers, nor offer writing instruction or advice nor do we accept or handle material for submission to production companies. Literary material should be submitted directly to the production companies or through a literary agent.

☐ Enclosed is a current list of literary agencies.

☐ Our Television Market List may be obtained by sending one dollar and addressing your request to the attention of Blanche Baker.

☐ Information on our Registration Service is enclosed.

☐ The minimum requirement for membership in the Guild is that you have had employment as a writer for screen, television, or radio or that you have sold original material to one of these media. The initiation fee is $300.00. Your application must be supported with a copy of your contract or other acceptable evidence of such employment or sale.

☐ For information on writing courses, we suggest you communicate with your State college or university or with your local Board of Education.

☐ Guild policy precludes us from giving out names, addresses, or phone numbers of any of our members. Correspondence may be addressed to a member in care of the Guild and will be forwarded promptly.

MANUSCRIPT REGISTRATION SERVICE

PURPOSE   The Guild's Registration Service has been set up to assist members and non-members in establishing the completion date and the identity of their literary property.

VALUE   Registration does not confer any statutory protection. It merely provides evidence of the writer's prior claim to authorship of the literary material involved and of the date of its completion. An author has certain rights under the law the moment his work is completed. It is therefore important that the date of completion be legally established. The Registration Office does not make comparisons of registration deposits to determine similarity between works, nor does it give legal opinions or advice.

COVERAGE   Since the value of registration is merely to supply evidence, it cannot protect what the law does not protect. Registration with the Guild does not protect titles (neither does registration with the United States Copyright Office).

PROCEDURE FOR DEPOSIT   Effective February 1, 1976 the following restrictions will be placed on material accepted for registration: One (1) copy, 8½ × 11 inch paper only, unbound. Use of one side only,

no onion skin paper and preferably white for best micro-film results. When it is received, the property is dated, given a registration
number and put on file. A receipt is returned. Notice of registration
shall consist of the wording REGISTERED WGAw NO._____and
be applied upon the title page or the page immediately following.
Formats, outlines, synopses or general descriptions of theatrical
motion pictures, radio and television programs are registrable.
Each property must be registered separately. (Exception: two episodes of an existing series may be deposited as a single registration.) Be sure that the name under which you register is your full
legal name. The use of pseudonyms, pen names or initials may
require proof of identity if you want to recover the material left on
deposit.

DURATION   The Guild reserves the right to micro-film the manuscript and to
destroy the manuscript at any time thereafter. You hereby autho-
rize the Guild to destroy the manuscript or the micro-film without
notice to you on the expiration of ten years from the date hereof.
You may however renew the registration for an additional ten years
if before the expiration of the first ten year period you pay the then
applicable renewal fee and get a written receipt therefor. Fee
should accompany request for renewal.

LOCATION OF REGISTRATION OFFICE:

9038 MELROSE AVENUE (at Doheny)
LOS ANGELES, CA 90069

HOURS: 10 A.M.–12 NOON
2 P.M.–5 P.M.   MONDAY THRU FRIDAY

PROCEDURE FOR WITHDRAWAL   The registered copy left on deposit cannot
be returned to the author without defeating the purpose of registration, the point being that evidence should be available, if necessary, that the material has been in the Guild's charge since the
date of deposit.

However, if the author finds it necessary to have the copy returned
to him, at least twenty-four (24) hours notice of intended withdrawal must be given to the Guild. If the manuscript is on micro-
film, a per page charge at then current rates will be made at time
of withdrawal. A manuscript will be surrendered only to the author
upon presentation of the original receipt and proper identification,
or, to another bearing a written authorization signed by the author.
Where there are co-authors, written consent of all parties must be
provided. And where the author is deceased, proof of death and
consent of heirs must be obtained. In no event, except under these
provisions, shall any of the material be allowed to be taken from
the Guild office unless a court order has been acquired.

If any person other than the author named in the registration shall request to see either the material deposited, the registration receipt, the registration envelope or any other material, such request shall be denied unless a court order is presented in connection therewith.

FEES $3.00 for members of WGA and WGGB
            $5.00 for non-members
            $1.00 for members when registration is renewed*
            $3.00 for members when registration is renewed**
            $1.50 for non-members when registration is renewed*
            $5.00 for non-members when registration is renewed**

*Registered prior to February 1, 1968
**Registered after February 1, 1968

NEW REGISTRATION FEES EFFECTIVE FEBRUARY 1, 1976

$4.00 for members of WGA and WGGB
$10.00 for non-members
$1.00 for members when registration is renewed*
$4.00 for members when registration is renewed**
$1.50 for non-members when registration is renewed*
$10.00 for non-members when registration is renewed**

*Registered prior to February 1, 1968
**Registered after February 1, 1968

FEE MUST ACCOMPANY REQUEST FOR REGISTRATION

GUILD FUNCTIONS AND SERVICES

1. CONTRACTS
   a. Negotiation of Basic Agreements in screen, television (both live and film), radio and staff agreements (news and continuity writers).
   b. Administration of same:
      (1) Handling of writer claims.
      (2) Checking of individual writer contracts for violations of the MBA.
      (3) Enforcement of Working Rules.
      (4) Processing of Grievances.

      (5) Distribution of Unfair Lists and Strike Lists.

      (6) Arbitrations under the MBA.

      (7) Collection and processing of television and motion picture residuals.

      (8) Pension Plan.

      (9) Health and Welfare Plan.

      (10) Signatory lists.

2. CREDITS

    a. Receipt of tentative notices.

    b. Arbitration of protests.

    c. Maintenance of Credit records.

    d. Distribution of Credits Manual.

    e. Credit information to members and to producers and agents.

3. ORIGINAL MATERIAL

    a. Registration.

    b. Collaboration Agreements.

    c. Settlement of disputes (Committee on Original Material).

    d. Copyright information and legislation.

4. AGENTS

    a. Negotiation of Basic Agreement with Agents.

    b. Recording, filing, and administration of individual agreements between writers and agents.

    c. Distribution of lists of authorized agents.

    d. Arbitration function in disputes between writers and agents.

5. EMPLOYMENT

    a. Compilation and distribution of TV Market Lists to members.

    b. Compilation and circulation of motion picture and TV credits lists to producers and agents.

    c. Compilation and circulation of statistical data re members where requested.

6. INFORMATION

    a. Inquiries by producers re member credits and contract provisions and agents.

    b. Inquiries by members and non-members re production data and contract provisions.

7. AFFILIATION AND COOPERATION

    a. British Writers Guild

    b. Australian Writers Guild

    c. Canadian Writers Guild

  d. Motion Picture and Television Relief Fund
  e. Permanent Charities Committee
  f. American Film Institute
  g. Open Door Program
  h. Other industry functions and services
 8. PUBLIC RELATIONS
  a. Publications—Newsletter
  b. Trade press
  c. TV forums
  d. Annual Awards Event
 9. CREDIT UNION
  a. Loans
  b. Investments
  c. Life Insurance
10. GROUP INSURANCE
  a. Life Insurance
  b. Disability; Hospitalization; Major Medical
11. LEGISLATION
  a. Copyright
  b. Censorship
  c. Taxation
  d. Unemployment Compensation
12. FILM SOCIETY
13. WORKSHOP PROGRAMS
14. SUPPORT OF FREEDOM OF EXPRESSION
  a. Litigation
  b. Press
  c. Other
15. DIRECTORY
16. COMMITTEES
  a. Writer Conferences
  b. Social Activities
17. WRITERS GUILD THEATRE
  a. Screenings (See Film Society)
  b. Rental
  c. Meeting Rooms

EXCERPTS—CONSTITUTION AND BY-LAWS

CONSTITUTION AND BY-LAWS
of the
WRITERS GUILD OF AMERICA, WEST, INC.

ARTICLE I

Name and Seal

The name of this corporation shall be the Writers Guild of America, West, Inc. Its seal shall be of a design adopted by its Board of Directors. Its principal office shall be in the County of Los Angeles, State of California.

ARTICLE II

Objects

The objects of this Guild are:

Section 1.   To promote and protect the professional and artistic interests of all creators and adaptors of literary, dramatic or musical material in the radio, television (live or film), motion picture industries and other related industries, as such industries are presently constituted or as they may hereafter be constituted or reconstituted as a result of any technical or scientific developments or discoveries as well as in pay television, cable television, compact devices or any other means of exhibition or distribution as yet unknown.

Section 2.   To represent members of the Guild for the purpose of collective bargaining.

Section 3.   To promote fair dealing and to cultivate, establish and maintain cordial relations, unity of action and understanding among all writers and to adjust, arbitrate, settle or otherwise resolve disputes relating to the work of members, their ownership of or other interests in written material; and to promote and cultivate fair dealings, cordial relations and understanding between this Guild, its members and other professional writers on the one hand, and organizations, groups or individuals with whom they have mutual aims or interests or with whom they work or have business or professional dealings, on the other hand.

Section 4.   To correct abuses to which members may be subjected; to assist members in securing equitable contracts, satisfactory working conditions and fair return in all dealings with employers and other with whom they have professional relations; and to establish and enforce standard minimum contracts and Codes of Fair Practice.

Section 5.   To stimulate an interest in and demand for, and to participate actively in, efforts to obtain adequate copyright legislation, both domestic and foreign, and to promote better copyright relations between the United States and other countries.

Section 6. To cooperate and/or enter into affiliation agreements where necessary with other groups or organizations having objectives or interests in common with the Guild.

Section 7. To protect the rights and property of the Guild and its members both at law and under the provisions of this Constitution and By-Laws; and to do any and all things necessary, desirable or proper to promote the welfare and interests of the Guild, its members and all professional writers, and to carry into effect or to further any of the foregoing purposes.

EXCERPTS—MEMBERSHIP

Section 1. General

There shall be four classes of membership in this Guild, which classes shall be denominated Associate, Current, Non-Current, and Withdrawn. Upon application to and acceptance in the Guild the applicant shall be designated either an Associate member or a Current member in accordance with the provisions of Sections 2 and 3 of this Article. In the event a member shall fail to maintain his Current membership in the Guild as provided in Section 4 of this Article, he shall nevertheless continue as a Non-Current member.

Section 2. Eligibility for Associate Membership

Any person engaged to write literary or dramatic material for, and any author of unpublished and unproduced literary or dramatic material as to which rights are sold or licensed or granted for use in the motion picture, radio, television industries or other related industries, as such industries are presently constituted or as they may hereafter be constituted or reconstituted, shall be eligible for Associate membership in this Guild.

Section 3. Eligibility for Current Status

The Unit Credit System hereafter set forth is designed to measure as accurately and fairly as possible the nature and kind of writing done. It shall be the duty of the Board of Directors to review the system and the designated units of credit from time to time. And when, in the judgment of the Board of Directors, changes occur in the industry or otherwise which warrant consideration by the membership, the Board of Directors shall place before the membership appropriate recommendations.

Any person shall attain Current status in the Guild if during the preceding two years he has accumulated an aggregate of twelve (12) Units of Credit as hereafter set forth, which units are based upon work completed under contract of employment or upon the sale or licensing of previously unpublished and unproduced literary or dramatic material provided, however, said employment, sale or licensing is within the jurisdiction of the Guild as provided in its collective bargaining contracts.

(a) If a person is employed within the Guild's jurisdiction on a week-to-week or term basis he shall be entitled to one Unit of Credit for each complete week of such employment.

(b) Units of Credit may also be attained in accordance with the following schedule:

<u>One Unit</u>

Episode in series for which writer receives "Created By" credit.
Comedy-Variety Program: one unit per week of employment or one unit per show, whichever is more.

<u>Two Units</u>

Story for theatrical motion picture short subject.
Story for TV or radio program one-half hour or less.

<u>Three Units</u>

Screenplay for theatrical motion picture short subject.
Teleplay or radio play for program one-half hour or less.
Television format or presentation for a new series.

<u>Four Units</u>

Story for one-hour TV or radio program.

<u>Five Units</u>

Story and teleplay or story and radio play one-half hour or less.

<u>Six Units</u>

Story for 90-minute teleplay or radio play.
One-hour teleplay or radio play.
Comedy-variety special regardless of length.

<u>Eight Units</u>

Story for theatrical motion picture.
Story for two-hour TV or radio program.

<u>Nine Units</u>

90-minute teleplay or radio play.

<u>Ten Units</u>

One-hour story and teleplay or story and radio play.

<u>Full Qualification for Current Status</u>

Screenplay for theatrical motion picture.
Two-hour teleplay or two-hour radio play.
90-minute story and teleplay or story and radio play.

(c) A rewrite is entitled to one-half the number of units allotted to its particular category in subdivision (b) above.

(d) A polish is entitled to one-quarter the number of units allotted to its particular category in subdivision (b) above.

(e) Sale of an option earns one-half the number of units allotted to its particular category in subdivision (b) above, subject to a maximum entitlement of four (4) such units in any one year.

(f) If a person under an employment contract writes material or sells or licenses previously unpublished or unproduced material intended as a pilot episode for a television series, he shall receive twice the number of units of credit applicable to similar material for a television program of equal length.

(g) Where writers collaborate on the same project each shall be accorded the appropriate number of units designated in subdivisions (b) through (f) above.

(h) All work done by a writer prior to acceptance into the Guild, in the case only of flat deal employment or sale of material, qualifies for one-half the applicable number of units in subdivisions (b) through (g) above for the purposes of achieving Current status. However in exceptional cases the Board of Directors, acting upon a recommendation of the Membership and Finance Committee, shall have power to grant the full number of units applicable in subdivisions (b) through (g).

(i) Unit credit for the writing or sale or licensing of material for pay television shall be determined by the Board of Directors. In addition, the Board of Directors shall have the authority, in any case not covered by this Section 3, to make specific Unit Credit determinations applicable to any such work. Unit Credit determinations made by the Board of Directors shall be submitted for approval by the membership at the first annual or special membership meeting following such determinations.

(j) For the sole purpose of determining Unit Credits where applicable the "Full Qualification" designation for screenplay for theatrical motion picture, two-hour teleplay or radio play and 90-minute story and teleplay or story and radio play, shall be deemed to be the equivalent of twelve (12) Units of Credit.

Section 4. Duration of Current Status
(a) Any Current member shall become a Non-Current member if, during any three consecutive years, he does not earn at least six (6) Units of Credit. A Non-Current member shall be reinstated to Current status if during any three (3) consecutive years as a Non-Current member, he earns six (6) Units of Credit. As of the date of adoption of this Constitution and thereafter, Current membership shall be extended one additional year for each six years of Current (or Active) membership in Writers Guild of America, West, Inc. or Writers Guild of America, East, Inc., provided, however, that such extensions will not be granted for a total of more than three years and will only apply to a member who is Current at the time they are granted. Additional years of extended Current membership shall not count in any calculation for a further extension.

(b) Any member with Current status who does not continue his Current status by reason of the foregoing provisions of this Section 4 shall maintain his Current status in the Guild for the sole purpose of participating in any voluntary member-paid insurance benefits which the Guild may presently or hereafter obtain.

EXCERPTS—WRITERS GUILD BASIC AGREEMENT OF 1973

Re: Writers Guild Basic Agreement of 1973

Gentlemen:

1. This letter constitutes a memorandum relating to the 1973 negotiations concerning the terms of employment of writers upon or for theatrical and television films. The provisions of this memorandum are stated in contract language except where the context clearly indicates otherwise.

In this memorandum the Writers Guild of America 1970 Theatrical and Television Film Basic Agreement for convenience is referred to simply as the "1970 WGA agreement"; the references to Articles and/or pages herein are as they appear in the 1970 WGA agreement.

2. In General

The terms and conditions of the Writers Guild of America 1973 Theatrical and Television Film Basic Agreement (hereafter simply "1973 WGA agreement") shall be the same as those contained in the 1970 WGA agreement as modified, changed and supplemented by this memorandum.

The preamble to the 1973 WGA agreement shall be as follows:

"This agreement, hereinafter referred to as 'Writers Guild of America 1973 Theatrical and Television Film Basic Agreement,' executed as of the 6th day of March, 1973, by and between Writers Guild of America, West, Inc. and Writers Guild of America, East, Inc. (hereinafter referred to as the 'Guild'), and the following producing member companies of the Association of Motion Picture and Television Producers, Inc.:

Article 1   Definitions

The following terms or words used herein shall have the following meaning:

A.   GENERAL

1. The term "television motion picture" (sometimes referred to in this Basic Agreement as "television film") means the entertainment portion of motion pictures, whether made on or by film, tape or otherwise and whether produced by means of motion picture cameras, electronic cameras or devices or any combination of the foregoing or any other means, methods or devices, now used or which may hereafter be adopted for the recordation of motion pictures produced primarily for exhibition by free television, excepting for the purpose of this Basic Agreement, kinescopes of live television broadcasts.

2. The term "theatrical motion picture" means motion pictures and photoplays, whether made on or by film, tape or otherwise and whether produced by means of motion picture cameras, electronic cameras, or devices or any combination of the foregoing or any other means, methods or devices now used or which may be hereafter adopted other than those motion pictures produced primarily for exhibition by free television.

3. The term "free television" means any method of exhibition by television of visual images but excluding "pay television."

4. The term "pay television" means a method of exhibition by television of a motion picture where a charge is paid by or assessed to or collected from the viewing audience, including subscription, telemeter or any other method whereby a charge is paid by the viewing audience for the right to view such motion picture.

5. The term "literary material" shall be deemed to include stories, adaptations, treatments, original treatment, scenarios, continuities, teleplays, screenplays, dialogue, scripts, sketches, plot, outlines, narrative synopses, routines, narrations and formats for use in the production of television film.

6. The term "radio rights" means the right to broadcast by radio for aural reception only and unaccompanied by any recordation, transmission or broadcast intended for visual reception.

7. "Week-to-Week Employment." Employment of a writer on a week-to-week basis is employment which, except for such restrictions as may herein elsewhere be contained, may be terminated by the Company or writer at any time.

8. The term "public domain" refers to literary material which is not subject to copyright protection in the United States.

9. A "member of the Guild in good standing" is defined as a member of the Guild who has tendered the initiation fee and periodic dues uniformly required as a condition of acquiring or retaining membership.

10. The term "writer" shall not be deemed to include any corporate or impersonal purveyor of literary material or rights therein.

11. Other than as provided in Article 14 hereof, this Basic Agreement shall not nor is it intended to cover the employment of Producers, Directors, Story Supervisors, Composers, Lyricists, or other persons employed in a bona fide non-writing capacity except to the extent that such employment consists of writing services covered under this Article 1, section B,1 (a) (2) and section C,1 (a) (3), nor the employment of Story Analysts, at any time prior to the expiration of this Basic Agreement, in the synopsizing of literary material, as referred to in subparagraph 1 (f) of the wage scales and working conditions of the current agreement between "Producer and I.A.T.S.E. & M.P.M.O. and Local #854 thereof."

12. It is understood that this Basic Agreement shall not, nor is it intended to cover (except as provided in Article 3 and 6) contracts solely for purchase of stories, or any person who writes, whether under an optional contract or otherwise on an independent contractor basis.

13. Other terms not expressly defined in this Basic Agreement are used in their present commonly understood meaning in the Motion Picture Industry in the State of California.

Article 1   Definitions
    1. Writer and Professional Writer
        a. A "writer" is a person who is:
            (i) engaged by the Company to write literary material as defined herein (including making changes or revisions in literary material), where the Company has the right by contract to direct the performance of personal ser-

vices in writing or preparing such material or in making revisions, modifications or changes therein; or

(ii) engaged by Company who performs services (at Company's direction or with its consent) in writing or preparing such literary material or making revisions, modifications, or changes in such material regardless of whether such services are described or required in his contract of employment.

A writer is a creative and professional person who performs a unique and indispensable function in relation to the production of motion pictures. It is an element of good faith, and part of the consideration of this agreement, that no company will use any of the following provisions of this paragraph with the purpose or intent of circumventing the employment of writers. Accordingly, it is agreed that the following services performed by an employee who is not employed as a writer shall not be subject to this agreement and such services shall not constitute such a person a writer hereunder:

(a) Cutting for time

(b) Bridging material necessitated by cutting for time

(c) Changes in technical or stage directions

(d) Assignment of lines to other existing characters occasioned by cast changes

(e) Changes necessary to obtain continuity acceptance or legal clearance

(f) Casual minor adjustments in dialogue or narration made prior to or during the period of principal photography

(g) Such changes in the course of production as are made necessary by unforeseen contingencies (e.g., the elements, accidents to performers, etc.)

(h) Instructions, directions or suggestions, whether oral or written, made to a writer regarding story or teleplay

In addition to the foregoing, if a person is employed solely in the capacity of the bona fide executive producer or bona fide producer of a specific television program and his employment agreement does not include the requirement that he perform writing services, and if said person has not been employed as a writer at least twice since June 1, 1966, and if said person nevertheless renders writing services (other than those specified in (a) through (h) above), then his employment as a writer shall be subject to this Basic Agreement, except that Article 6. and Article 14. of this Basic Agreement shall not be applicable if he performs no more than the following writing services on not more than three programs in any one production season (not more than one of which may be a program in a mini-series, which for this purpose is a series of not more than 8 episodes in the production season): changes in dialogue, narration or action, but not including significant changes in plot, story line or interrelationship of characters. If such person makes significant changes in plot, story line or interrelationship of characters, such person shall be subject to Articles 6. and 14. of this Basic Agreement. In determining whether a person has been employed as a writer since June 1,

1966, for the purposes of this subparagraph, (i) each separate occasion, if any, for which he has declared earnings to the Guild for services as a writer performed on a particular theatrical motion picture or television project since June 1, 1966, and (ii) each occasion, if any, on which he has been listed as a participating writer in relation to a screen authorship credit determination pursuant to a collective bargaining agreement with the Guild with respect to services performed as a writer since June 1, 1966, shall be conclusively counted as an employment as a writer.

b. A "professional writer" means any person who has (a) received employment for a total of 13 weeks as a television, motion picture or radio writer, or (b) has received credit on the screen as a writer for a television or theatrical motion picture, or (c) has received credit for three (3) original stories or one (1) teleplay for a program one-half hour or more in length in the field of live television, or (d) has received credit for three (3) radio scripts for radio programs one-half hour or more in length, or (e) has received credit for one professionally produced play on the legitimate stage or one published novel.

EXCERPTS—GUILD SHOP (GENERAL)

Article 6   Guild Shop—(GENERAL)

1. Except as provided below, in both theatrical and television films each writer employed by Company on the effective date of this Basic Agreement who is then a member of the Guild in good standing shall remain a member in good standing, and each writer so employed who is not a member shall, on or before the thirtieth day following the effective date of this Basic Agreement, become and remain a member of the Guild in good standing. Each writer employed hereunder by Company after the effective date of this Basic Agreement shall not later than the thirtieth day following the beginning of his first employment, as hereinafter defined, in the motion picture and television industry, become and remain a member of the Guild in good standing.

The term "first employment" as referred to above shall mean the first such employment to which the provisions of this Basic Agreement apply as a writer for a motion picture by an employer in the motion picture and television industry, on or after the effective date of this Basic Agreement.

2. The provisions of subsection 1. of this Article 6 shall not apply

a. If a writer is not a member of the Guild at the time of his employment and although required by the provisions of his employment agreement to do so, fails or refuses to become a member of the Guild in good standing within the 30 days abovementioned, provided that within 15 days after written notice thereof from the Guild to the Company, the Company shall either terminate such employment or shall pay or cause to be paid the initiation fees and dues of the writer in the manner, within the time, and subject to the provisions of subsection 5.b. hereof relating to the payment of dues. If the Company elects to and does pay such initiation fees and dues, such writer shall be deemed to be a member of the Guild in good standing, but only for the period necessary to permit him to complete the performance of his services in connection with the then current assignment. The Company may use this exception only once for any particular person.

b. To a writer whom the Company is required to employ as a condition of the sale or license of material, provided that within 15 days after written notice from the Guild to the Company that such writer is not a member of the Guild in good standing, the Company shall either terminate such employment, or shall pay or cause to be paid the initiation fees and dues that the writer would otherwise be required to pay hereunder during such employment, in the manner, within the time, and subject to the provisions of subsection 5.b. hereof relating to the payment of dues. However, the writers employed by the Company within the exception provided for in this subparagraph (b) shall not exceed 10% of the total number of writers in the employ of the Company. For the purpose of such computation if the Company has in its employ at any time less than 10 writers, then 1 of such writers so employed may fall within this exception. Promptly following the employment of any writer claimed by the Company to be within this exception, the Company will notify the Guild in writing of the name of the writer employed, the date of the employment agreement and the fact that the Company claims that such writer is an exception hereunder. For the purpose of such computation a writer who is employed under an exclusive contract by a Company shall be regarded as being employed by the Company at all times during the term of such contract, including periods during which the writer may be on layoff and periods during which such contract may be suspended by reason of illness or default of the writer or otherwise. The writer shall be regarded as continuing in the employ of the Company by which he is employed regardless of the fact that his services may be loaned to another Company.

Paragraph 5 is deleted and the following Paragraph 5 is substituted in its place and stead:

5. If during any time that a writer is employed by the Company under a contract of employment such writer is or becomes a member of the Guild in good standing and if such writer shall subsequently and before his employment under such contract terminates, cease to be a member of the Guild in good standing then:

a. If such writer has ceased or shall cease to be a member for any reason other than his failure to pay dues, such writer shall, for the purposes of this Basic Agreement, be deemed to remain a member of the Guild in good standing throughout the writer's employment under said contract of employment as the same may be extended or renewed pursuant to any provisions or options therein contained.

b. If he has ceased or shall cease to be a member in good standing by reason of his failure to pay dues, and if the Guild gives the Company written notice of that fact within three business days after such writer is first named on the weekly list provided for in Article 3 A.1. of this Basic Agreement.

EXCERPTS—GENERAL PROVISIONS

A. <u>GENERAL PROVISIONS</u>
  1. <u>Term of Agreement</u>
     The term of this contract is from March 6, 1973 through March 1, 1977.
B. <u>SEPARATED RIGHTS AND WRITER'S RIGHTS</u>
   <u>SCREEN</u>
  1. The maximum price a writer must pay a Company for abandoned material is limited to the total writing costs the Company has incurred.
  2. When a theatrical film is re-made, the original writers will now be covered as participating writers and, if they receive credit, will share in any television release money.
  3. Screen writers must now be *invited* to sneak previews.
  4. There is a $500 penalty for shopping material to any Company proscribed by the writer.
   <u>TELEVISION</u>
  1. Creators of episodic-type material for comedy-variety and other unit series programs (e.g. "The Bickersons") will receive a sequel payment of not less than $175.00 per episode.
  2. Upset prices are increased as follows:

	Old Rate	New Rate
30 minute story & teleplay	$12,500	$15,000
60 minute story & teleplay	$18,500	$22,500
90 minute (or longer) story & teleplay	$23,500	$28,000
Format only	$ 6,500	$ 7,500

  3. The writer who creates an unique principal character in any new series I receive $100 for each subsequent episode in which such character appears.
  4. Creators of material (e.g. "All in the Family") that is used on phonograph records, etc. will be entitled to 25% of the Company's net receipts from the licensing of such material.
  5. When a television film is released theatrically in a foreign market only, the Company must pay 100% of either the theatrical or television minimum, whichever is higher. If such film is released either domestically or world-

wide, the payment is either 150% of television minimums or 100% of theatrical minimum, whichever is higher. These minimums are in addition to any initial compensation paid to the writer.

6. The original writer of a television film that is re-made must receive the full minimum compensation he would have received had he been employed under our current contract, such minimum to be based on the credit.

7. Writers on unit series or one-time shows where there are no separated rights will receive compensation for merchandising and publication of the script in the same manner as the writer of an episode of a series.

8. Writers of pilots and one-time shows must be advised—without asking— of the names of all other writers working on the same project.

9. The Company may no longer use a telephone call as à method of frustrating the provision that a commitment is deemed made if there are two meetings on the same story.

10.Unless the writer authorizes the Company to submit unpublished material there is a penalty of $500. for each third party to which the material is submitted.

C. CREDITS

Television

1. The companies agree that in their licensing and distribution agreements they will require the licensee to exhibit all the writing credits as they appear on the screen.

2. The "created by" credit must be on a separate card and contiguous to the writer's credit.

3. A "developed by" credit may be given only to a person who has contributed to the writing on the particular program or series.

4. A story editor must receive a credit in a form approved by the Guild, on a separate card.

5. Under our old Agreement the Company's obligation to have credits determined by the Guild ceased in the event of a work stoppage. Under the new Agreement all work done during a contract term is subject to credit determination by the Guild. This applies to credits during the 1973 strike and covers screen as well as television.

Screen

6. The Company must include the writing credit in all publicity, handouts, screening invitations, etc., if the names of the individual producer and director are included, even if such credit is in the form of a presentation or production credit.

Where a "presentation" or "production" credit is given in advertising to any one individual, the writer's credit must be 75% of the size and in the same style of type as such credit. If there are two or more production or presentation credits, the writer's credit must be 100% of the size, and in the same style of type, as the largest such credit.

WGA 1977 THEATRICAL AND TELEVISION BASIC AGREEMENT
THEATRICAL COMPENSATION

EMPLOYMENT, FLAT DEALS **

	Effective 3/2/77 - 3/1/79		Effective 3/2/79 - 3/1/80		Effective 3/2/80 - 3/1/81	
	LOW	HIGH	LOW	HIGH	LOW	HIGH
A. Screenplay, Including Treatment	$11,211	$20,821	$12,220	$22,695	$14,175	$26,326
Installments:						
Delivery of Treatment	4,204	6,406	4,582	6,983	5,315	8,100
Delivery of First Draft Screenplay	5,046	9,610	5,500	10,475	6,380	12,151
Delivery of Final Draft Screenplay	1,961	4,805	2,138	5,237	2,480	6,075
B. Screenplay, Excluding Treatment	$ 7,008	$14,414	$ 7,639	$15,711	$ 8,861	$18,225
Installments:						
Delivery of First Draft Screenplay	5,046	9,610	5,500	10,475	6,380	12,151
Delivery of Final Draft Screenplay	1,962	4,804	2,139	5,236	2,481	6,074
C. Additional Compensation for Story Included in Screenplay	$ 1,602	$ 3,203	$ 1,746	$ 3,491	$ 2,025	$ 4,050
D. Story or Treatment	$ 4,204	$ 6,406	$ 4,582	$ 6,983	$ 5,315	$ 8,100
E. Original Treatment	$ 5,806	$ 9,610	$ 6,329	$10,475	$ 7,342	$12,151
F. First Draft Screenplay, With or Without Option For Final Draft Screenplay						
First Draft Screenplay	$ 5,046	$ 9,610	$ 5,500	$10,475	$ 6,380	$12,151
Final Draft Screenplay	$ 3,363	$ 6,406	$ 3,666	$ 6,983	$ 4,253	$ 8,100
G. Rewrite of Screenplay	$ 4,204	$ 6,406	$ 4,582	$ 6,983	$ 5,315	$ 8,100
H. Polish of Screenplay	$ 2,102	$ 3,203	$ 2,291	$ 3,491	$ 2,658	$ 4,050

* LOW BUDGET — Photoplay costing less than $1,000,000
  HIGH BUDGET — Photoplay costing $1,000,000 or more

* For special minimum terms applicable to Low Budget photoplays, see page 2.
** Explanation on discounts on page 3.

WGA 1977 THEATRICAL AND TELEVISION BASIC AGREEMENT

THEATRICAL COMPENSATION

SPECIAL MINIMUM TERMS APPLICABLE TO LOW BUDGET PHOTOPLAYS (under $1,000,000)

For details as to applicability of the special Low Budget schedule, contact the Guild.

EMPLOYMENT, FLAT DEALS

	Effective 3/2/77 - 3/1/78		Effective 3/2/78 - 3/1/79	Effective 3/2/79 - 3/1/80	Effective 3/2/80 - 3/1/81
	Minimum Compensation	Additional Sum Payable on Start of Principal Photography			
A. Screenplay, Including Treatment	$10,611	$720	$11,407	$12,377	$14,172
Installments:					
Delivery of Treatment	3,979		4,277	4,641	5,314
Delivery of First Draft Screenplay	4,775		5,133	5,569	6,377
Delivery of Final Draft Screenplay	1,857		1,997	2,167	2,481
B. Screenplay, Excluding Treatment	$ 6,632	$451	$ 7,129	$ 7,735	$ 8,857
Installments:					
Delivery of First Draft Screenplay	4,775		5,133	5,569	6,377
Delivery of Final Draft Screenplay	1,857		1,996	2,166	2,480
C. Additional Compensation for Story Included in Screenplay	$ 1,516	$103	$ 1,630	$ 1,769	$ 2,026
D. Story or Treatment	$ 3,979	$271	$ 4,277	$ 4,641	$ 5,314
E. Original Treatment	$ 5,495	$373	$ 5,907	$ 6,409	$ 7,338
F. First Draft Screenplay, With or Without Option for Final Draft Screenplay					
First Draft Screenplay	$ 4,775	$325	$ 5,133	$ 5,569	$ 6,377
Final Draft Screenplay	$ 3,183	$216	$ 3,422	$ 3,713	$ 4,251
G. Rewrite of Screenplay	$ 3,979	$271	$ 4,277	$ 4,641	$ 5,314
H. Polish of Screenplay	$ 1,990	$135	$ 2,139	$ 2,321	$ 2,658

WGA 1977 THEATRICAL AND TELEVISION BASIC AGREEMENT
THEATRICAL COMPENSATION

** The MBA provides for a discount with respect to employment on a flat deal
basis of a writer who has not been previously employed in television,
theatrical films or dramatic radio, subject to an adjustment to full minimum
if a photoplay is produced utilizing such writer's material. For details,
contact the Guild.

PAYMENT SCHEDULE

Upon commencement of writing services, writer is to be paid, as an advance, not
less than: (a) 10% of the agreed installment which is payable on delivery of the
first material; or, (b) $968 (effective 3/2/77 - 3/1/79), $1,055 (effective 3/2/79 -
3/1/80) or $1,224 (effective 3/2/80 - 3/1/81), whichever is greater. Balance
"payable on delivery" of material is to be paid within 48 hours after delivery.
Payment shall not be contingent upon the acceptance or approval of the Company or
upon any other contingency such as the obtaining of financing.

PURCHASES FROM A PROFESSIONAL WRITER

The Flat Deal minimums shall apply to purchases of literary material
from a "professional writer" as that term is specifically defined in the Basic
Agreement.

TELEVISION RELEASE PRIOR TO THEATRICAL RELEASE

If a writer is employed at a theatrical minimum, and the picture is released on free
TV before being released theatrically, the writer must receive a salary adjustment
so that the higher of either the theatrical or television minimum is paid.

WEEK-TO-WEEK AND TERM EMPLOYMENT

Compensation Per Week *	Effective 3/2/77 - 3/1/79	Effective 3/2/79 - 3/1/80	Effective 3/2/80 - 3/1/81
Week-to-week	$1,043	$1,137	$1,319
14 out of 14 weeks	968	1,055	1,224
20 out of 26 weeks	894	974	1,130
40 out of 52 weeks	821	895	1,038

* The MBA provides for a discount for a limited period of time with respect
to employment on a week-to-week or term basis of a writer who has not
been previously employed in television, theatrical films or dramatic radio.
For details, contact the Guild.

WGA 1977 THEATRICAL AND TELEVISION BASIC AGREEMENT
THEATRICAL COMPENSATION

NARRATION (written by a writer other than writer of Screenplay or Story & Screenplay)

Minimums for narration are based on status of film assembly and nature of previously written material as follows:

Nature of Material Written prior to employment of narration writer	Film Assembled in Story Sequence	Film Footage Not Assembled in Story Sequence
None	Applicable Screenplay excluding Treatment Minimum	Applicable Screenplay including Treatment Minimum
Story Only	Applicable Screenplay excluding Treatment Minimum	Applicable Screenplay excluding Treatment Minimum
Story and Screenplay	Per Rate Schedule A	Per Rate Schedule A

	Effective 3/2/77 – 3/1/79	Effective 3/2/79 – 3/1/80	Effective 3/2/80 – 3/1/81
Rate Schedule A			
Two minutes or less	$197	$215	$249
Over two minutes thru five minutes	693	755	876
Over five minutes	Applicable Polish Minimum		

All employment under the WGA 1977 Theatrical and Television Basic Agreement is subject to employer contributions of:

5% to the PRODUCER-WRITERS GUILD OF AMERICA PENSION PLAN; and
4% to the WRITERS GUILD-INDUSTRY HEALTH FUND.

Employer reporting forms and information regarding benefits are available from the Pension Plan and Health Fund offices located at:

310 No. San Vicente Boulevard
Los Angeles, California 90048
PHONE: (213) 659-6430 (Pension) / (213) 659-7100

WGA 1977 THEATRICAL AND TELEVISION BASIC AGREEMENT
TELEVISION COMPENSATION

Length of Program: 30 minutes or less (but more than 15 minutes)

HIGH BUDGET MINIMUMS ($27,500 & over)

	Effective 3/2/77 – 3/1/78	Effective 3/2/78 – 3/1/79	Effective 3/2/79 – 3/1/80	Effective 3/2/80 – 3/1/81
APPLICABLE MINIMUMS				
STORY-----------------------	$1,046	$1,130	$1,220	$1,330
TELEPLAY--------------------	$1,699	$1,835	$1,982	$2,160

Installments:
   * First Draft: 60% of Agreed Compensation but
    not less than 90% of minimum
  Final Draft: Balance of Agreed Compensation				

STORY & TELEPLAY------------	$2,614	$2,823	$3,049	$3,323

Installments:
   * Story: 30% of Agreed Compensation
  First Draft Teleplay: 40% of Agreed
   Compensation or the difference between
   the Story Installment and 90% of minimum,
   whichever is greater
  Final Draft Teleplay: Balance of Agreed
   Compensation				

**GOING RATE-----------------	$3,710	$4,007	$4,328	$4,718
**BONUS----------------------	$1,590	$1,717	$1,854	$2,021

* On pilots only, the writer is to be paid 10% of the first installment (as an advance against such first installment) upon commencement of services. The applicable minimum for a pilot story or story and teleplay is 150% of the applicable minimum set forth above.

IF THE GOING RATE AND BONUS ARE APPLICABLE, TOTAL
COMPENSATION FOR STORY AND TELEPLAY IS:

Effective	
3/2/77–3/1/78	$5,300
3/2/78–3/1/79	$5,724
3/2/79–3/1/80	$6,182
3/2/80–3/1/81	$6,739

** The GOING RATE and BONUS are applicable to Stories and/or Teleplays for Network Prime Time. For a detailed explanation, refer to page 9.

3/77

WGA 1977 THEATRICAL AND TELEVISION BASIC AGREEMENT
TELEVISION COMPENSATION

Length of Program: 60 minutes or less (but more than 30 minutes)

HIGH BUDGET MINIMUMS ($52,250 & over)

	Effective 3/2/77 – 3/1/78	Effective 3/2/78 – 3/1/79	Effective 3/2/79 – 3/1/80	Effective 3/2/80 – 3/1/81
APPLICABLE MINIMUMS				
STORY-----------------------	$1,901	$2,053	$2,217	$2,417
TELEPLAY--------------------	$3,293	$3,556	$3,840	$4,186

Installments:
* First Draft: 60% of Agreed Compensation but
  not less than 90% of minimum
Final Draft: Balance of Agreed Compensation

STORY & TELEPLAY------------	$4,753	$5,133	$5,544	$6,043

Installments:
* Story: 30% of Agreed Compensation
First Draft Teleplay: 40% of Agreed
Compensation or the difference between
the Story Installment and 90% of minimum,
whichever is greater
Final Draft Teleplay: Balance of Agreed
Compensation

**GOING RATE (Story & Teleplay)-	$4,770	$5,152	$5,564	$6,065
(Story, Option for Teleplay)--	$5,194	$5,609	$6,057	$6,603
**BONUS----------------------	$2,650	$2,862	$3,091	$3,369

* On pilots only, the writer is to be paid 10% of the first installment (as an
  advance against such first installment) upon commencement of services.

IF THE GOING RATE AND BONUS ARE APPLICABLE, TOTAL
COMPENSATION FOR STORY AND TELEPLAY IS:

Effective	Story & Teleplay	Story, Option for Teleplay
3/2/77-3/1/78	$7,420	$7,844
3/2/78-3/1/79	$8,014	$8,471
3/2/79-3/1/80	$8,655	$9,148
3/2/80-3/1/81	$9,434	$9,972

** The GOING RATE and BONUS are applicable to Stories and/or Teleplays for
Network Prime Time. For a detailed explanation, refer to page 9.

WGA 1977 THEATRICAL AND TELEVISION BASIC AGREEMENT
TELEVISION COMPENSATION

Length of Program: 90 minutes or less (but more than 75 minutes)

HIGH BUDGET MINIMUMS ($92,000 & over)

	Effective 3/2/77 – 3/1/78	Effective 3/2/78 – 3/1/79	Effective 3/2/79 – 3/1/80	Effective 3/2/80 – 3/1/81
APPLICABLE MINIMUMS				
STORY-----------------------	$2,756	$2,976	$3,214	$3,503
TELEPLAY--------------------	$4,884	$5,275	$5,697	$6,210

Installments:
* First Draft: 60% of Agreed Compensation but
  not less than 90% of minimum
Final Draft: Balance of Agreed Compensation

STORY & TELEPLAY------------	$6,890	$7,441	$8,036	$8,759

Installments:
* Story: 30% of Agreed Compensation
First Draft Teleplay: 40% of Agreed
  Compensation or the difference between
  the Story Installment and 90% of minimum,
  whichever is greater
Final Draft Teleplay: Balance of Agreed
  Compensation

**GOING RATE------------------	$7,950	$8,586	$9,273	$10,108
**BONUS-----------------------	$2,650	$2,862	$3,091	$ 3,369

* On pilots and non-episodic programs, the writer is to be paid 10% of the first
  installment (as an advance against such first installment) upon commencement
  of services. The applicable minimum for a pilot story or story and teleplay is
  150% of the applicable minimum set forth above.

IF THE GOING RATE AND BONUS ARE APPLICABLE, TOTAL
COMPENSATION FOR STORY AND TELEPLAY IS:

Effective	
3/2/77-3/1/78	$10,600
3/2/78-3/1/79	$11,448
3/2/79-3/1/80	$12,364
3/2/80-3/1/81	$13,477

** The GOING RATE and BONUS are applicable to Stories and/or Teleplays for
   Network Prime Time. For a detailed explanation refer to page 9 .

WGA 1977 THEATRICAL AND TELEVISION BASIC AGREEMENT
TELEVISION COMPENSATION

Length of Program: 120 minutes or less (but more than 90 minutes)

HIGH BUDGET MINIMUMS($125,000 & over)

	Effective 3/2/77 - 3/1/78	Effective 3/2/78 - 3/1/79	Effective 3/2/79 - 3/1/80	Effective 3/2/80 - 3/1/81
APPLICABLE MINIMUMS				
STORY-----------------------	$3,611	$3,900	$ 4,212	$ 4,591
TELEPLAY---------------------	$6,479	$6,997	$ 7,557	$ 8,237

Installments:
* First Draft: 60% of Agreed Compensation but
   not less than 90% of minimum
Final Draft: Balance of Agreed Compensation

STORY & TELEPLAY------------	$9,028	$9,750	$10,530	$11,478

Installments:
* Story: 30% of Agreed Compensation
First Draft Teleplay: 40% of Agreed
  Compensation or the difference between
  the Story Installment and 90% of minimum,
  whichever is greater
Final Draft Teleplay: Balance of Agreed
  Compensation

**GOING RATE (Story & Teleplay)-	$ 9,540	$10,303	$11,127	$12,128
(Story, Option for Teleplay)--	$10,090	$10,897	$11,769	$12,828
**BONUS----------------------	$ 3,710	$ 4,007	$ 4,328	$ 4,718

* On pilots and non-episodic programs, the writer is to be paid 10% of the first
installment (as an advance against such first installment) upon commencement
of services. The applicable minimum for a pilot story or story and teleplay is
150% of the applicable minimum set forth above.

IF THE GOING RATE AND BONUS ARE APPLICABLE, TOTAL
COMPENSATION FOR STORY AND TELEPLAY IS:

Effective	Story & Teleplay	Story, Option for Teleplay
3/2/77-3/1/78	$13,250	$13,800
3/2/78-3/1/79	$14,310	$14,904
3/2/79-3/1/80	$15,455	$16,097
3/2/80-3/1/81	$16,846	$17,546

** The GOING RATE and BONUS are applicable to Stories and/or Teleplays for
Network Prime Time. For a detailed explanation, refer to page 9 .

WGA 1977 THEATRICAL AND TELEVISION BASIC AGREEMENT
TELEVISION COMPENSATION

Length of Program: 15 minutes or less

HIGH BUDGET MINIMUMS ($16,500 & over)

	Effective 3/2/77 - 3/1/78	Effective 3/2/78 - 3/1/79	Effective 3/2/79 - 3/1/80	Effective 3/2/80 - 3/1/81
APPLICABLE MINIMUMS				
STORY----------------------	$ 571	$ 617	$ 666	$ 726
TELEPLAY--------------------	$1,046	$1,130	$1,220	$1,330

Installments:
* First Draft: 60% of Agreed Compensation but
  not less than 90% of minimum
Final Draft: Balance of Agreed Compensation

STORY & TELEPLAY------------	$1,428	$1,542	$1,665	$1,815

Installments:
* Story: 30% of Agreed Compensation
First Draft Teleplay: 40% of Agreed
  Compensation or the difference between
  the Story Installment and 90% of minimum,
  whichever is greater
Final Draft Teleplay: Balance of Agreed
  Compensation

** EXPLANATION OF GOING RATE & BONUS APPLICABLE TO STORIES AND/OR TELEPLAYS
OF 30 MINUTES OR MORE IN LENGTH FOR NETWORK PRIME TIME:

The GOING RATE shall be paid for the writing of both story and teleplay,
whether by option or otherwise, for programs intended for network prime time,
to writers who have previously written at least twice within the genre (drama
or comedy) of the particular program, or who have written at least once within
the genre and were compensated therefore in an amount equal to the going rate.

The BONUS shall be paid for the writing of the story and teleplay for programs
intended for network prime time. If the teleplay is written by a freelance
writer from a story written by another writer, the teleplay writer shall receive
60% of the bonus and the story writer shall receive 40%. If the teleplay is
written by a term contract writer from a story by a freelance writer, the teleplay
share of the bonus will be paid to the Writers Guild-Industry Health Fund.

WGA 1977 THEATRICAL AND TELEVISION BASIC AGREEMENT

TELEVISION COMPENSATION

HIGH BUDGET MINIMUMS

REWRITE - APPLICABLE MINIMUMS	Effective 3/2/77 - 3/1/78	Effective 3/2/78 - 3/1/79	Effective 3/2/79 - 3/1/80	Effective 3/2/80 - 3/1/81
15 minutes or less	$ 617	$ 666	$ 719	$ 784
30 minutes or less (more than 15)	1,029	1,111	1,200	1,308
60 minutes or less (more than 30)	1,948	2,104	2,272	2,476
75 minutes or less (more than 60)	2,733	2,952	3,188	3,475
90 minutes or less (more than 75)	2,868	3,097	3,345	3,646
120 minutes or less (more than 90)	3,788	4,091	4,418	4,816

POLISH - APPLICABLE MINIMUMS

15 minutes or less	$ 308	$ 333	$ 360	$ 392
30 minutes or less (more than 15)	514	555	599	653
60 minutes or less (more than 30)	974	1,052	1,136	1,238
75 minutes or less (more than 60)	1,366	1,475	1,593	1,736
90 minutes or less (more than 75)	1,433	1,548	1,672	1,822
120 minutes or less (more than 90)	1,893	2,044	2,208	2,407

PLOT OUTLINE - NARRATIVE SYNOPSIS OF STORY

Company may request writer to prepare a narrative synopsis of plot outline of a story owned by writer to determine its suitability for television. Company has 14 days from delivery to elect to acquire the outline and to employ the writer. If Company does not proceed, the outline and all right, title and interest therein is retained by writer.

APPLICABLE MINIMUMS

15 minutes or less	$ 285	$ 308	$ 333	$ 363
30 minutes or less (more than 15)	476	514	555	605
60 minutes or less (more than 30)	903	975	1,053	1,148
75 minutes or less (more than 60)	1,177	1,271	1,373	1,497
90 minutes or less (more than 75)	1,331	1,437	1,552	1,697
120 minutes or less (more than 90)	1,759	1,900	2,052	2,237

BACK-UP SCRIPTS

Applicable minimum compensation for a "Back-Up Script" (story and/or teleplay) is 115% of the compensation set forth herein for story and/or teleplay.

FORMAT --------------------------	$1,978	$2,136	$2,307	$2,515
BIBLE for Multi-Part Series---- ----	$10,000	$10,800	$11,664	$12,714
plus, for each storyline in				
excess of six (6) ----------------	$ 1,000	$ 1,080	$ 1,166	$ 1,271

(a discount of 20% is applicable if "bible" is intended for Non-Network or Non-Prime Time)

WGA 1977 THEATRICAL AND TELEVISION BASIC AGREEMENT
TELEVISION COMPENSATION

HIGH BUDGET MINIMUMS

NARRATION

Minimums for narration are based on status of film assembly and nature of previously written material as follows:

Nature of Material Written Prior to Employment of Narration Writer	Film Assembled in Story Sequence	Film Footage Not Assembled in Story Sequence
None	Rate Schedule A	Rate Schedule B
Story Only	Rate Schedule A	Rate Schedule A
Story and Teleplay	Rate Schedule C	Rate Schedule C

RATE SCHEDULE A

Program Length	Effective 3/2/77 - 3/1/78	Effective 3/2/78 - 3/1/79	Effective 3/2/79 - 3/1/80	Effective 3/2/80 - 3/1/81
15 minutes or less	$1,235	$1,334	$1,441	$1,571
30 minutes or less (more than 15)	2,055	2,219	2,397	2,613
60 minutes or less (more than 30)	3,899	4,211	4,548	4,957
75 minutes or less (more than 60)	5,464	5,901	6,373	6,947
90 minutes or less (more than 75)	5,743	6,202	6,698	7,301
120 minutes or less (more than 90)	7,585	8,192	8,847	9,643

RATE SCHEDULE B

Program Length				
15 minutes or less	$1,428	$1,542	$ 1,665	$ 1,815
30 minutes or less (more than 15)	2,612	2,821	3,047	3,321
60 minutes or less (more than 30)	4,753	5,133	5,544	6,043
75 minutes or less (more than 60)	6,534	7,057	7,622	8,308
90 minutes or less (more than 75)	6,891	7,442	8,037	8,760
120 minutes or less (more than 90)	9,029	9,751	10,531	11,479

RATE SCHEDULE C

2 minutes or less of narration	$ 197	$ 213	$ 230	$ 251
2 to 5 minutes of narration	693	748	808	881
Over 5 minutes of narration	Rewrite minimum for applicable program lengt

WGA 1977 THEATRICAL AND TELEVISION BASIC AGREEMENT
TELEVISION COMPENSATION

NETWORK PRIME TIME RERUNS

As to stories and/or teleplays written on or after 3/2/78, compensation payable for all reruns on a network in prime time is payable at the following percentages of applicable minimum:

Material written After:	DATE OF RERUN	
	"In Season" (Sep. 1 thru May 4)	"Out of Season" (May 5 thru Aug. 31)
March 2, 1978	90%	70%
March 2, 1979	100%	80%

OTHER RERUN COMPENSATION

The minimum compensation payable with respect to reruns in the United States and Canada is as follows:

2nd Run	50% of applicable minimum if on a network; otherwise, 40%
3rd Run	40% of applicable minimum if on a network; otherwise, 30%
4th 5th 6th } Run	25% of applicable minimum for each such run
7th 8th 9th 10th } Run	15% of applicable minimum for each such run
11th 12th } Run	10% of applicable minimum for each such run

13th Run and each run thereafter – 5% of applicable minimum for each such run.

PRIME TIME VARIETY RERUN COMPENSATION, ONCE PER WEEK OR LESS

Compensation for reruns shall be computed as follows:

2nd Run	100% of applicable aggregate minimum
3rd Run	75% of applicable aggregate minimum
4th 5th } Run	50% of applicable aggregate minimum for each such run
6th Run	25% of applicable aggregate minimum
7th Run	10% of applicable aggregate minimum

Each subsequent run – 5% of applicable aggregate minimum for each such run.

Which compensation is allocated among the credited writers.

WGA 1977 THEATRICAL AND TELEVISION BASIC AGREEMENT
TELEVISION COMPENSATION

FOREIGN TELECAST COMPENSATION

Initial Foreign Telecast   15% of applicable minimum

When foreign gross exceeds:
  $ 7,000 on 30 minute film ⎤
  $13,000 on 60 minute film ⎬   Additional 10% of applicable minimum
  $18,000 on longer film   ⎦

When foreign gross exceeds:
  $10,000 on 30 minute film ⎤
  $18,000 on 60 minute film ⎬   Additional 10% of applicable minimum
  $24,000 on longer film   ⎦

COMEDY/VARIETY FOREIGN TELECAST COMPENSATION

When calculating foreign telecast compensation for prime time variety programs
originally broadcast once per week or less, the applicable story and teleplay
minimums are to be substituted for the applicable comedy/variety minimums.

WEEK-TO-WEEK AND TERM EMPLOYMENT

WRITER-Compensation Per Week*	Effective 3/2/77 - 3/1/78	Effective 3/2/78 - 3/1/79	Effective 3/2/79 - 3/1/80	Effective 3/2/80 - 3/1/81
Week-to-week	$ 832	$ 899	$ 971	$1,058
6 out of 6 weeks	832	899	971	1,058
14 out of 14 weeks guarantee	772	834	901	982
20 out of 26 weeks guarantee	712	769	831	906
40 out of 52 weeks guarantee	653	705	761	829

* The MBA provides for a discount for a limited period of time with respect
to employment on a week-to-week or term basis of a writer who has not
been previously employed in television, theatrical films or dramatic radio.
For details, contact the Guild.

WRITER EMPLOYED IN ADDITIONAL
CAPACITIES-Compensation Per Week

Week-to-week & Term Employment up to and including 9 weeks	$1,551	$1,675	$1,809	$1,972
10 to 19 week guarantee	1,292	1,395	1,507	1,643
20 weeks or more guarantee	1,163	1,256	1,356	1,478

  -Program Fees

30-minute Program	$ 194	$ 210	$ 227	$ 247
60-minute Program	259	280	302	329
90-minute Program or Longer	323	349	377	411

WGA 1977 THEATRICAL AND TELEVISION BASIC AGREEMENT
TELEVISION COMPENSATION

NON-COMMERCIAL OPENINGS & CLOSINGS

Aggregate Running Time of Material	Effective 3/2/77 - 3/1/78	Effective 3/2/78 - 3/1/79	Effective 3/2/79 - 3/1/80	Effective 3/2/80 - 3/1/81
3 minutes or less	$ 514	$ 555	$ 599	$ 653
More than 3 minutes	721	779	841	917

PURCHASES OF LITERARY MATERIAL

The minimums are applicable to purchases of previously unexploited material from a "Professional Writer" (as defined in the Basic Agreement).

SEQUEL PAYMENTS

If a Company commences exploitation of the television sequel (i.e., series) rights in connection with material to which separation of rights applies, the writer or writers entitled to separation of rights must be paid not less than the following sequel payments for each sequel episode:

Series of:	Effective 3/2/77 - 3/1/78	Effective 3/2/78 - 3/1/79	Effective 3/2/79 - 3/1/80	Effective 3/2/80 - 3/1/81
15-minute episodes	$222.60	$ 240.60	$ 259.80	$ 283.20
30-minute episodes	371.00	401.00	433.00	472.00
60-minute episodes	704.90	761.90	822.70	896.80
90-minute or longer episodes	927.50	1,002.50	1,082.50	1,180.00

CHARACTER "SPIN-OFF" PAYMENTS

Character "Spin-off" payments equal to the above sequel payments are payable to the writer who introduces a new character in a serial, episodic, anthology or one-time show if such character becomes the central character in a new serial or episodic series.

RECURRING CHARACTER PAYMENTS

Recurring character payments are payable to the writer who introduces a new character in an episodic series for each episode in which such character appears in the following amounts:

Effective	
3/2/77 - 3/1/78	$106
3/2/78 - 3/1/79	114
3/2/79 - 3/1/80	123
3/2/80 - 3/1/81	134

3/77

WGA 1977 THEATRICAL AND TELEVISION COMPENSATION
THEATRICAL COMPENSATION

LOW BUDGET MINIMUMS	Effective 3/2/77 – 3/1/78	Effective 3/2/78 – 3/1/79	Effective 3/2/79 – 3/1/80	Effective 3/2/80 – 3/1/81
STORY				
15 minutes or less	$ 487	$ 526	$ 568	$ 619
30 minutes or less (more than 15)	808	873	943	1,028
60 minutes or less (more than 30)	1,530	1,652	1,784	1,945
90 minutes or less (more than 75)	2,251	2,431	2,625	2,861
120 minutes or less (more than 90)	2,972	3,210	3,467	3,779
TELEPLAY				
15 minutes or less	$ 762	$ 823	$ 889	$ 969
30 minutes or less (more than 15)	1,309	1,414	1,527	1,664
60 minutes or less (more than 30)	2,497	2,697	2,913	3,175
90 minutes or less (more than 75)	3,688	3,983	4,302	4,689
120 minutes or less (more than 90)	4,881	5,271	5,693	6,205
STORY & TELEPLAY				
15 minutes or less	$1,213	$1,310	$1,415	$1,542
30 minutes or less (more than 15)	2,020	2,182	2,357	2,569
60 minutes or less (more than 30)	3,826	4,132	4,463	4,865
90 minutes or less (more than 75)	5,626	6,076	6,562	7,153
120 minutes or less (more than 90)	7,431	8,025	8,667	9,447
REWRITE				
15 minutes or less	$ 452	$ 488	$ 527	$ 574
30 minutes or less (more than 15)	772	834	901	982
60 minutes or less (more than 30)	1,472	1,590	1,717	1,872
90 minutes or less (more than 75)	2,175	2,349	2,537	2,765
120 minutes or less (more than 90)	2,876	3,106	3,354	3,656
POLISH				
15 minutes or less	$ 225	$ 243	$ 262	$ 286
30 minutes or less (more than 15)	385	416	449	489
60 minutes or less (more than 30)	737	796	860	937
90 minutes or less (more than 75)	1,089	1,176	1,270	1,384
120 minutes or less (more than 90)	1,439	1,554	1,678	1,829

All employment under the WGA 1977 Theatrical and Television Basic Agreement is
subject to employer contributions of:

5% to the PRODUCER-WRITERS GUILD OF AMERICA PENSION PLAN; and
4% to the WRITERS GUILD-INDUSTRY HEALTH FUND.

Employer reporting forms and information regarding benefits are available from the
Pension Plan and Health Fund offices located at:
310 No. San Vicente Boulevard
Los Angeles, California 90048

PHONE: (213) 659-6430 (Pension) / (213) 659-7100 (Health)

WGA 1977 THEATRICAL AND TELEVISION BASIC AGREEMENT
TELEVISION COMPENSATION

COMEDY-VARIETY PROGRAMS

APPLICABLE PROGRAM MINIMUMS Length or Time Bracket	Effective 3/2/77 - 3/1/78	Effective 3/2/78 - 3/1/79	Effective 3/2/79 - 3/1/80	Effective 3/2/80 - 3/1/81
5 minutes	$ 339	$ 366	$ 395	$ 431
10 minutes	675	729	787	858
15 minutes	953	1,029	1,111	1,211
30 minutes	2,067	2,232	2,411	2,628
45 minutes	2,243	2,422	2,616	2,851
60 minutes	2,843	3,070	3,316	3,614
75 minutes	3,310	3,575	3,861	4,208
90 minutes	3,876	4,186	4,521	4,928

ONE PROGRAM PER WEEK,
MINIMUM VARIETY SHOW COMMITMENT

If all writers on a once-per-week variety series are employed under a contract
providing for guaranteed employment in cycles of thirteen (13) or more weeks, the
applicable weekly minimum for each such writer is:

Effective	
3/2/77 - 3/1/78	$750
3/2/78 - 3/1/79	810
3/2/79 - 3/1/80	875
3/2/80 - 3/1/81	954

and the aggregate minimum compensation for each program is:

Number of Writers	Percentage of Applicable Program Minimums
1	100%
2	150%
3	175%
4	200%

plus 25% for each additional writer.

-16-

WGA 1977 THEATRICAL AND TELEVISION BASIC AGREEMENT
TELEVISION COMPENSATION

FIVE PROGRAMS PER WEEK, MINIMUM VARIETY SHOW COMMITMENT

If all writers on a five-per-week variety series are employed under a contract providing for guaranteed employment in cycles of thirteen (13) or more weeks, the aggregate minimum compensation for each weekly unit of programs is as follows:

Effective 3/2/77 - 3/1/78

Length or Time Bracket	1	2	3	4	5
10 minutes (Prime Time)	$2,614	$2,851	$3,329		
(Non-Prime)	2,091	2,281	2,663		
15 minutes (Prime Time)		3,660	4,135	$ 4,611	
(Non-Prime)		2,928	3,308	3,689	
30 minutes (Prime Time)			6,181	6,774	$ 7,369
(Non-Prime)			4,945	5,419	5,895
60 minutes (Prime Time)				11,645	12,238
(Non-Prime)				9,316	9,790

Effective 3/2/78 - 3/1/79

Length or Time Bracket	1	2	3	4	5
10 minutes (Prime Time)	$2,823	$3,079	$3,595		
(Non-Prime)	2,258	2,463	2,876		
15 minutes (Prime Time)		3,953	4,466	$ 4,980	
(Non-Prime)		3,162	3,573	3,984	
30 minutes (Prime Time)			6,675	7,316	$ 7,959
(Non-Prime)			5,340	5,853	6,367
60 minutes (Prime Time)				12,577	13,217
(Non-Prime)				10,062	10,574

Effective 3/2/79 - 3/1/80

Length or Time Bracket	1	2	3	4	5
10 minutes (Prime Time)	$3,049	$3,325	$3,883		
(Non-Prime)	2,439	2,660	3,106		
15 minutes (Prime Time)		4,269	4,823	$ 5,378	
(Non-Prime)		3,415	3,858	4,302	
30 minutes (Prime Time)			7,209	7,901	$ 8,596
(Non-Prime)			5,767	6,321	6,877
60 minutes (Prime Time)				13,583	14,274
(Non-Prime)				10,866	11,419

(cont)

WGA 1977 THEATRICAL AND TELEVISION BASIC AGREEMENT
TELEVISION COMPENSATION

FIVE PROGRAMS PER WEEK,
MINIMUM VARIETY SHOW COMMITMENT (cont)

Effective 3/2/80 - 3/1/81

Length or Time Bracket		1	2	Number of Writers 3	4	5
10 minutes	(Prime Time)	$3,323	$3,624	$4,232		
	(Non-Prime)	2,658	2,899	3,386		
15 minutes	(Prime Time)		4,653	5,257	$ 5,862	
	(Non-Prime)		3,722	4,206	4,690	
30 minutes	(Prime Time)			7,857	8,612	$ 9,370
	(Non-Prime)			6,286	6,890	7,496
60 minutes	(Prime Time)				14,805	15,559
	(Non-Prime)				11,844	12,447

The applicable weekly minimum for each writer is:

Effective	
3/2/77 - 3/1/78	$750
3/2/78 - 3/1/79	810
3/2/79 - 3/1/80	875
3/2/80 - 3/1/81	954

WGA 1977 THEATRICAL AND TELEVISION BASIC AGREEMENT
TELEVISION COMPENSATION

COMEDY-VARIETY PROGRAMS (cont)

DISCOUNTS FOR NON-CANCELLABLE CONTRACTS

For any writer who is employed under a term contract non-cancellable for
thirteen (13) or more weeks, the applicable weekly minimum is subject to a
ten percent (10%) discount. For any writer who is employed under a term
contract non-cancellable for twenty-six (26) or more weeks, the applicable
weekly minimum is subject to a twenty percent (20%) discount. If all writers
on a variety series are employed under term contracts non-cancellable for
thirteen (13) or more weeks, the applicable program minimums are subject to
a ten percent (10%) discount. If all of the writers on a variety series are
employed under term contracts non-cancellable for twenty-six (26) or more
weeks, the applicable program minimums are subject to a twenty percent (20%)
discount.

MINIMUMS FOR PRE-PRODUCTION PERIODS
FOR WRITERS EMPLOYED UNDER MINIMUM VARIETY SHOW COMMITMENT

	Compensation Per Week			
	Effective 3/2/77 - 3/1/78	Effective 3/2/78 - 3/1/79	Effective 3/2/79 - 3/1/80	Effective 3/2/80 - 3/1/81
First and Second Weeks	$525.00	$567.00	$612.50	$667.80
Third and Fourth Weeks	600.00	648.00	700.00	763.20
Fifth and Sixth Weeks	675.00	729.00	787.50	858.60
Thereafter	750.00	810.00	875.00	954.00

SKETCH MINIMUMS

Prime Time	$700.00	$756.00	$816.00	$889.00
Non-Prime Time	560.00	605.00	653.00	711.00

LYRICS UNACCOMPANIED BY MUSIC

$551.00	$595.00	$643.00	$701.00

APPLICABLE TIME PERIOD

Where less than fifty percent (50%) of a variety program consists of material
written by writers, the applicable minimum shall be the minimum applicable to
the time period actually consumed by the material but not less than the minimum
time bracket indicated:

	Minimum Time Bracket	
Length of Program	Prime Time Once Per Week	Other
15 minutes or less	10 minutes	10 minutes
30 minutes or less	15 minutes	15 minutes
60 minutes or less	30 minutes	15 minutes
Over 60 minutes	30 minutes	30 minutes

WGA 1977 THEATRICAL AND TELEVISION BASIC AGREEMENT
TELEVISION COMPENSATION

QUIZ AND AUDIENCE PARTICIPATION

APPLICABLE MINIMUM PER WEEKLY UNIT
OF NOT MORE THAN FIVE (5) PROGRAMS

Guarantee	Effective 3/2/77 - 3/1/78	Effective 3/2/78 - 3/1/79	Effective 3/2/79 - 3/1/80	Effective 3/2/80 - 3/1/81
Less than 14 weekly units	$563	$608	$657	$716
14, but less than 20 weekly units	523	565	610	665
20, but less than 39 weekly units	481	519	561	611
39 or more weekly units	443	478	516	562

WRITERS OF QUESTIONS, ANSWERS AND/OR IDEAS FOR STUNTS WHERE
SUCH WRITER SUPPLIES NO OTHER MATERIAL

To be negotiated separately with packagers of Quiz and Audience Participation
programs.

WEEKLY UNIT OF SIX (6) PROGRAMS

180% of above minimums, if weekly unit includes one program for broadcast
on a network in prime time.

Otherwise, 150% of above minimums.

WGA 1977 THEATRICAL AND TELEVISION BASIC AGREEMENT
TELEVISION COMPENSATION

SERIALS, OTHER THAN PRIME TIME

Aggregate Minimum For Each Weekly Unit Of Five (5) Serial Programs

	Effective 3/2/77 - 3/1/78	Effective 3/2/78 - 3/1/79	Effective 3/2/79 - 3/1/80	Effective 3/2/80 - 3/1/81
15 minutes	$2,331	$2,518	$2,719	$2,964
30 minutes	3,885	4,196	4,532	4,940
45 minutes	5,633	6,084	6,571	7,163
60 minutes	7,187	7,763	8,384	9,139

Script Fee

For each script on which a writer performs writing services, such writer
will be paid not less than:

15 minutes	$ 231	$ 250	$ 269	$ 293
30 minutes	385	416	449	489
45 minutes	558	603	651	709
60 minutes	712	770	831	905

"TRIAL PERIOD" Script Fee

The minimum Script Fee for a trial period (limited to an aggregate of six (6) weeks
during a thirteen (13) week period) is 80% of the applicable Script Fee above.

LONG TERM STORY PROJECTION

The minimum for a long term story projection (when written by a writer other
than a Head Writer) for a non-prime time serial is:

Effective	
3/2/77 - 3/1/78	$5,000
3/2/78 - 3/1/79	5,400
3/2/79 - 3/1/80	5,832
3/2/80 - 3/1/81	6,357

WGA 1977 THEATRICAL AND TELEVISION BASIC AGREEMENT
TELEVISION COMPENSATION

OTHER NON-PRIME TIME, NON-DRAMATIC PROGRAMS,
RELIGIOUS PROGRAMS, WHETHER OR NOT DRAMATIC

	Effective 3/2/77 - 3/1/78	Effective 3/2/78 - 3/1/79	Effective 3/2/79 - 3/1/80	Effective 3/2/80 - 3/1/81
Originals				
5 minutes	$ 296	$ 320	$ 346	$ 377
10 minutes	591	638	689	751
15 minutes	835	902	974	1,062
30 minutes	1,671	1,805	1,949	2,124
45 minutes	1,963	2,120	2,290	2,496
60 minutes	2,503	2,703	2,919	3,182
75 minutes	2,898	3,130	3,380	3,684
90 minutes	3,534	3,817	4,122	4,493
Adaptations				
5 minutes	$ 236	$ 255	$ 275	$ 300
10 minutes	445	481	519	566
15 minutes	668	721	779	849
30 minutes	1,179	1,273	1,375	1,499
45 minutes	1,444	1,560	1,685	1,837
60 minutes	1,867	2,016	2,177	2,373
75 minutes	2,063	2,228	2,406	2,623
90 minutes	2,602	2,810	3,035	3,308

STANDARD FORM FREELANCE TELEVISION WRITER'S EMPLOYMENT CONTRACT

Agreement entered into at _____,
this _____ day of _____, 19 _____ between _____,
hereinafter called "Company" and _____
hereinafter called "Writer."

WITNESSETH:

1. Company hereby employs the Writer to render services in the writing, composition, preparation and revision of the literary material described in Paragraph 2 hereof, hereinafter for convenience referred to as "work." The Writer accepts such employment and agrees to render his services hereunder and devote his best talents, efforts and abilities in accordance with the instructions, control and directions of the Company.

2. DESCRIPTION OF WORK
   (a) IDENTIFICATION
   Series Title: _____
   Program Title: _____
   Based on _____
   (b) FORM
   ( ) Story   ( ) Option for Teleplay
   ( ) Teleplay   ( ) Pilot
   ( ) Rewrite   ( ) Polish
   ( ) Sketch   ( ) Narration
   ( ) Format
   ( ) Non Commercial Openings and Closings
   ( ) Plot Outline—Narrative Synopsis of Story
   (c) TYPE OF PROGRAM
   ( ) Episodic Series   ( ) Unit Series   ( ) Single Unit
   (d) PROGRAM LENGTH: _____ minutes
   (e) METHODS OF PRODUCTION & DISTRIBUTION
   ( ) Film   ( ) Videotape   ( ) Live
   ( ) Network   ( ) Syndication

3. (a) The Writer represents that (s)he is a member in good standing of the Writers Guild of America (West or East), Inc., and warrants that he will maintain such membership in good standing during the term of his employment.
   (b) The Company warrants it is a party to the Writers Guild of America 1973 Basic Agreement (which agreement is herein designated MBA).
   (c) Should any of the terms hereof be less advantageous to the Writer than the minimums provided in said MBA, then the terms of the MBA shall supersede such terms hereof; and in the event this Agreement shall fail to provide benefits for the Writers which are provided by the MBA, then such

benefits for the Writer provided by the terms of the MBA are deemed incorporated herein. Without limiting the generality of the foregoing, it is agreed that screen credits for authorship shall be determined pursuant to the provisions of Schedule A of the MBA in accordance with its terms at the time of such determination.

4. DELIVERY:

If the Writer has agreed to complete and deliver the work, and/or any changes and revisions, within a certain period or periods of time, then such agreement will be expressed in this paragraph as follows:

5. COMPENSATION:

As full compensation for all services to be rendered hereunder, the rights granted to the Company with respect to the work, and the undertakings and agreements assumed by the Writers, and upon condition that the Writer shall fully perform such undertakings and agreements, Company will pay the Writer the following amounts:

    (a) Compensation for services $ _____
    (b) Advance for television reruns $ _____
    (c) Advance for theatrical use $ _____

No amounts may be inserted in (b) or (c) above unless the amount set forth in (a) above is at least twice the applicable minimum compensation set forth in the MBA for the type of services to be rendered hereunder.

If the assignment is for story and teleplay, story with option for teleplay or teleplay the following amounts of the compensation set forth in (a) above will be paid in accordance with the provisions of the MBA:

    (i) $_____following delivery of story.
    (ii) $_____following delivery of first draft teleplay.
    (iii) $_____following delivery of final draft teleplay.

6. RIGHT TO OFFSET:

With respect to Writer's warranties and indemnification agreement, the Company and the Writer agree that upon the presentation of any claim or the institution of any action involving a breach of warranty, the party receiving notice thereof will promptly notify the other party in regard thereto. Company agrees that the pendency of any such claim or action shall not relieve the Company of its obligation to pay the Writer any monies until it has sustained a loss or suffered an adverse judgment or decree by reason of such claim or action.

IN WITNESS WHEREOF, the parties hereto have duly executed this agreement on the day and year first above written.

_____   ·   _____
          (Writer)   (Company)

Address _____   By _____

Title _____
Address _____
_____
_____

INDEPENDENT PRODUCERS

A & S PRODUCTIONS, INC.
(THE) ALPHA CORPORATION
AMERICAN INTERNATIONAL PRODUCTIONS,
  A CALIFORNIA CORPORATION
ARTANIS PRODUCTIONS, INC.
AUBREY SCHENCK ENTERPRISES, INC.
BING CROSBY PRODUCTIONS, INC.
BRIEN PRODUCTIONS, INC.
BRISTOL PRODUCTIONS, INC.
CHARLESTON ENTERPRISES CORPORATION
CHRISLAW PRODUCTIONS, INC.
COLUMBIA PICTURES INDUSTRIES, INC.
DAISY PRODUCTIONS, INC.
DANNY THOMAS PRODUCTIONS
DARR-DON, INC.
EDPROD PICTURES, INC.
FILMWAYS, INC.
FORMOSA PRODUCTIONS, INC.
FOUR STAR INTERNATIONAL, INC.
FRANK ROSS PRODUCTIONS
GEOFFREY PRODUCTIONS, INC.
GIBRALTAR PRODUCTIONS, INC.
HANNA-BARBERA PRODUCTIONS, INC.
HAROLD HECHT COMPANY
HERBERT LEONARD ENTERPRISES, INC.
JACK CHERTOK TELEVISION, INC.
JACK ROLLINS AND CHARLES H. JOFFEE
  PRODUCTIONS
(THE) KAPPA CORPORATION
LAWRENCE TURMAN, INC.
LEGARLA, INC.
LEONARD FILMS, INC.
LEVY-GARDNER-LAVEN PRODUCTIONS, INC.
LUCILLE BALL PRODUCTIONS, INC.

(THE) MALPASO COMPANY
MAX E. YOUNGSTEIN ENTERPRISES, INC.
METEOR FILMS, INC.
METRO-GOLDWYN-MAYER INC.
METROMEDIA PRODUCERS CORPORATION
MILLFIELD PRODUCTIONS, INC.
(THE) MIRISCH CORPORATION OF
   CALIFORNIA
MIRISCH FILMS, INC.
MIRISCH PRODUCTIONS, INC.
MOTION PICTURES INTERNATIONAL, INC.
MURAKAMI WOLF PRODUCTIONS INC.
NGC TELEVISION INC.
NORLAN PRODUCTIONS, INC.
OAKMONT PRODUCTIONS, INC.
PARAMOUNT PICTURES CORPORATION
PAX ENTERPRISES, INC.
PAX FILMS, INC.
RAINBOW PRODUCTIONS, INC.
RASTAR ENTERPRISES, INC.
RASTAR PRODUCTIONS, INC.
RFB ENTERPRISES, INC.
R.F.D. PRODUCTIONS
ROBERT B. RADNITZ PRODUCTIONS, LTD
SHELDON LEONARD PRODUCTIONS
(THE) STANLEY KRAMER CORPORATION
STUART MILLAR PRODUCTIONS, INC.
SUMMIT FILMS, INC.
T & L PRODUCTIONS, INC.
THOMAS/SPELLING PRODUCTIONS
TWENTIETH CENTURY-FOX FILM CORP.
UNIVERSAL CITY STUDIOS, INC.
WALT DISNEY PRODUCTIONS
WARNER BROS. INC.
WOLPER PICTURES, LTD.
WRATHER CORPORATION

WRITERS' REPRESENTATIVES

Unless otherwise stated, all addresses are in Los Angeles, California.

ABRAMS-RUBALOFF & ASSOCIATES
273-5711
9012 Beverly Blvd. (90048)
ADAMS, BRET, LIMITED 656-6420
8282 Sunset Blvd. (90046)
36 E. 61st St., (212) 752-7864
New York, New York (10021)
ADAMS, RAY & ROSENBERG
278-3000
9200 Sunset Blvd., PH 25
(90069)
AIMEE ENTERTAINMENT
ASSOCIATION 872-0374
14241 Ventura Blvd., 990-6996
Sherman Oaks, Calif. (91423)
ALVARADO, CARLOS, AGENCY
652-0272
8820 Sunset Blvd. (90069)
AMBER, VELVET, AGENCY
464-8184
6515 Sunset Blvd., Suite 200A
(90028)
AMSEL, FRED & ASSOCIATES
277-2035
312 S. Beverly Dr., Suite R,
Beverly Hills, Calif. (90212)
ARCARA, BAUMAN & HILLER
ARTISTS' MANAGERS 271-5601
9220 Sunset Blvd. (90069)
850 7th Ave., Suite 1201
New York, New York (10019)
(212) 757-0098
ARTISTS CAREER MANAGEMENT
278-9157

9157 Sunset Blvd., #206
(90069)
ASSOCIATED BOOKING
CORPORATION 273-5600
9595 Wilshire Blvd., Beverly
Hills, Calif. (90212)
BARR, RICKEY/GILLY, GEORGIA
659-0141
8721 Sunset Blvd., Suite 210
(90069)
BARSKIN AGENCY, THE 657-5740
8730 Sunset Blvd., Suite #501
(90069)
BART/LEVY ASSOCIATES, INC.
550-1060
9169 Sunset Blvd. (90069)
BEAKEL & JENNINGS AGENCY
ARTISTS' MANAGERS 274-5418
9615 Brighton Way, Suite 314
Beverly Hills, Calif. (90210)
BELCOURT ARTISTS . . 276-6205
222 N. Canon Dr., Suite 204
Beverly Hills, Calif. (90210)
BELLEVUE LITERARY AGENCY
478-9470
Kirkeby Center, Suite 1034
10889 Wilshire Blvd. (90024)
BLAKE, WILLIAM, AGENCY/WEST
TALENT INTERNATIONAL
274-0321
1888 Century Park East
(90067)
BLOOM, BECKETT, LEVY & SHORR
553-4850

449 S. Beverly Dr., Beverly
Hills, Calif. (90212)

BLUMENTHAL ARTISTS AGENCY
656-1451
435 S. La Cienega Blvd.
(90048)

BRADY, CHRISTINA, AGENCY
473-2708
11818 Wilshire Blvd. (90025)

BRAND AGENCY. . . .   657-2870
8721 Sunset Blvd. (90069)

BRANDON & BARAD ASSOCIATES
273-6173
9046 Sunset Blvd. (90069)

BRESLER, WOLFF, COTA &
LIVINGSTON   278-3200
190 N. Canon Dr., Beverly
Hills, Calif. (90210)

BREWIS, ALEX, AGENCY   274-9874
8721 Sunset Blvd. (90069)

BRIDGETOWN MUSIC
CORPORATION   333-5288
283-1830
723½ N. Glendora Ave.,
La Puente, Calif. (91744)

BROWN, NED, INCORPORATED
276-1131
407 N. Maple Dr., Suite 228,
Beverly Hills, Calif. (90210)

CALDER AGENCY, THE   652-3380
8749 Sunset Blvd. (90069)

CAMBRIDGE COMPANY, THE
657-2125
9000 Sunset Blvd.,   666-1920
Suite 814 (90069)

CARTER AGENCY, INC., THE
277-2683
1801 Avenue of the Stars, Suite
640 (90067)

CENTURY ARTISTS, LTD. 273-4366

9744 Wilshire Blvd., Suite 206
Beverly Hills, Calif. (90212)

CHANDLER, RITA, AGENCY
656-4042
8282 Sunset Blvd. (90046)

CHARTER MANAGEMENT 278-1690
9000 Sunset Blvd. (90069)

CHARTWELL ARTISTS, LTD.
553-3600
1901 Avenue of the Stars
(90067)

CHASIN-PARK-CITRON AGENCY
273-7190
9255 Sunset Blvd. (90069)

COLLIER, SHIRLEY, AGENCY
270-4500
1127 Stradella Rd. (90024)
(Representatives in all foreign
countries)

COLTON, KINGSLEY &
ASSOCIATES, INC. . .   277-5491
321 S. Beverly Dr., Beverly
Hills, Calif. (90212)

COMPASS MANAGEMENT, INC.
271-5122
211 S. Beverly Dr.
Beverly Hills, Calif. (90212)

CONNOR-CORFINO, ASSOCIATES,
INC.   981-1133
14241 Ventura Blvd. Sherman
Oaks, Calif. (91423)

CONTEMPORARY-KORMAN
ARTISTS, LTD.   278-8250
Contemporary Artists Building
132 Lasky Dr., Beverly Hills,
Calif. (90212)

CONWAY, BEN & ASSOC. 271-8133
999 N. Doheny Dr., # 403
(90069)

COOPER, DOUG, AGENCY 980-6100

10850 Riverside Dr., Suite
601-A
N. Hollywood, Calif. (91602)
CORALIE JR. AGENCY 766-9501
4789 Vineland 681-8281
N. Hollywood, Calif. (91602)
COSAY, WERNER & ASSOCIATES
550-1535
9744 Wilshire Blvd.,
Beverly Hills, Calif. (90212)
CREATIVE ARTISTS AGENCY, INC.
277-4545
1888 Century Park East, Suite
1400 (90067)
CUMBER, LIL, ATTRACTIONS
AGENCY. 469-1919
6515 Sunset Blvd., Suite 408
(90028)
DADE/ROSEN ASSOCIATES
278-7077
999 N. Doheny Dr., Suite 102
(90069)
DANSON ARTISTS' AGENCY
769-3100
10732 Riverside Dr.,
N. Hollywood, Calif. (91602)
DIAMOND ARTISTS, LTD.
654-5960
8400 Sunset Blvd. (90069)
119 W. 57th St.,
(212) CI7-3025
New York, New York (10019)
EISENBACH-GREENE-DUCHOW,
INC. 659-3420
760 N. La Cienega Blvd.
(90069)
FCA AGENCY, INC. . . 278-1460
9000 Sunset Blvd. (90069)
FERRELL, CAROL, AGENCY
466-8311

6331 Hollywood Blvd., #828
(90028)
FIELDS, JACK & ASSOCIATES
278-1333
9255 Sunset Blvd., Suite 1105
(90069)
FILM ARTISTS MANAGEMENT
ENTERPRISES, INC.. . 656-7590
8278 Sunset Blvd. (90046)
FISCHER, SY, COMPANY, THE
273-3575
9255 Sunset Blvd. (90069)
FLEMING, PETER, AGENCY
271-5693
9046 Sunset Blvd., Suite 206
(90069)
GARRICK, DALE, INTERNATIONAL
AGENCY. 657-2661
8831 Sunset Blvd. (90069)
GERSH, PHIL, AGENCY, INC.
274-6611
222 N. Canon Dr., Beverly
Hills, Calif. (90210)
GIBSON, CARTER J., AGENCY
274-8813
9000 Sunset Blvd. (90069)
GOLDFARB/LEWIS AGENCY
659-5955
Falcon Gold, Inc.
8733 Sunset Blvd. (90069)
GOLDSTEIN, ALLEN & ASSOC.,
LTD.. 278-5005
9301 Wilshire Blvd., Beverly
Hills, Calif. (90210)
GORDEAN-FRIEDMAN AGENCY,
INC., THE 273-4195
9229 Sunset Blvd. (90069)
GRANITE AGENCY, THE 934-8383
1920 S. La Cienega Blvd., Suite
205 (90034)

GRASHIN, MAURI, AGENCY
                 652-5168
8730 Sunset Blvd. (90069)
GREEN, IVAN, AGENCY, THE
                 277-1541
1900 Avenue of the Stars, Suite
1070 (90067)
GREENE, GLORIA, CREATIVE
EXPRESSIONS   274-7661
439 La Cienega Blvd. (90048)
GROSSMAN, LARRY &
ASSOCIATES, INC. . .   550-8127
9229 Sunset Blvd., Suite 502
(90069)
GROSSMAN-STALMASTER AGENCY
                 657-3040
8730 Sunset Blvd., Suite 405
(90069)
HALLIBURTON, JEANNE, AGENCY
                 466-6138
5205 Hollywood Blvd., Suite
203 (90027)
HALSEY, REECE, AGENCY
652-2409
8733 Sunset Blvd. (90069)
                 652-7595
HAMILBURG, MITCHELL J.,
AGENCY.   657-1501
292 S. La Cienega Blvd., Suite
212,
Beverly Hills, Calif. (90211)
HENDERSON/HOGAN AGENCY,
INC.   274-7815
247 S. Beverly Dr., Beverly
Hills, Calif. (90212)
200 W. 57th St. (212) 765-5190
New York, New York (10019)
HOLLYWOOD, DANIEL,
THEATRICAL MANAGEMENT,
LTD..   550-0570

9200 Sunset Blvd., Suite 808
(90069)
HUSSONG, ROBERT G., AGENCY,
INC.   655-2534
8271 Melrose Ave., Suite 108
(90046)
HYLAND-DE LAUER, LITERARY
AGENCY.   278-0300
8961 Sunset Blvd. (90069)
I.M. AGENCY LTD. . .   277-1376
1888 Century Park East
(90067)
INTERNATIONAL CREATIVE
MANAGEMENT   550-4000
8899 Beverly Blvd. (90048)
40 West 57th Street,
New York, New York (10019)
                 (212) 556-5600
INTERNATIONAL LITERARY
AGENTS, LTD.   274-8779
Peri Winkler
9601 Wilshire Blvd., Suite 300,
Beverly Hills, Calif. (90210)
IRWIN, LOU, AGENCY   553-4775
9901 Durant Dr., Suite A,
Beverly Hills, Calif. (90212)
ISER, BEVERLY KAHN, AGENCY
                 657-8693
9701 Wilshire Blvd., Suite 710
Beverly Hills, Calif. (90212)
JACKSON, IONE J. . . .   293-8833
4306 S. Crenshaw Blvd.
(90008)
JOSEPH, L.H. JR. & ASSOCIATES
                 651-2322
8344 Melrose Ave. (90069)
KAHN-PENNEY AGENCY 656-4042
8282 Sunset Blvd. (90046)
KANE, MERRILY, AGENCY
                 550-8874

9171 Wilshire Blvd.,
Suite 310,
Beverly Hills, Calif. (90210)
KARLIN, LARRY, AGENCY
550-0570
9200 Sunset Blvd. (90069)
KOHNER, PAUL-LEVY, MICHAEL
AGENCY. 550-1060
9169 Sunset Blvd. (90069)
KURLAND, NORMAN, AGENCY,
THE 274-8921
9701 Wilshire Blvd.,
Suite 800
Beverly Hills, Calif. (90212)
LARSEN, MICHAEL-POMADA,
ELIZABETH, LITERARY AGENTS
(415) 673-0939
1029 Jones St.,
San Francisco, Calif. (94109)
LAZAR, IRVING PAUL, AGENCY
275-6153
211 S. Beverly Dr.,
Beverly Hills, Calif. (90212)
LENNY, JACK, ASSOCIATES
271-2174
9701 Wilshire Blvd., Beverly
Hills, Calif. (90212)
140 W. 58th Street,
New York, New York (10019)
(212) 582-0270
LEVEE, GORDON B., AGENCY
652-0012
8721 Sunset Blvd., Suite 103
(90069)
LEVERING, LILLIA ARTISTS'
MANAGER 874-9591
P.O. Box 1447 (90028)
LEWIS, HENRY, AGENCY
275-5129
9172 Sunset Blvd. (90069)

LITTMAN, ROBERT, COMPANY,
THE 278-1572
409 N. Camden Drive, Beverly
Hills, Calif. (90210)
LOO, BESSIE, AGENCY 657-5888
8746 Sunset Blvd. (90069)
LOVELL & ASSOCIATES 659-8476
8730 Sunset Blvd. (90069)
LYONS, GRACE, AGENCY
652-5290
8732 Sunset Blvd. (90069)
MAJOR TALENT AGENCY, INC.
820-5841
12301 Wilshire Blvd., Suite 515
(90025)
MARKSON, RAYA L. LITERARY
AGENCY. 552-2083
Artists' Manager 997-6699
788-6788
1888 Century Park East,
Suite 1015 (90067)
MCCLENDON, ERNESTINE,
ENTERPRISES, INC.. . 654-4425
8440 Sunset Blvd., Suite M-5
(90069)
MCHUGH, JAMES, AGENCY
651-2770
8150 Beverly Blvd., Suite 206
(90048)
MCKIERNAN & GURROLA
746-3550
1150 S. Olive St., Suite 1400
(90015)
MEDFORD, BEN, AGENCY 271-7021
9440 Santa Monica Blvd.,
Suite 403 (92120)
MEIKLEJOHN, WILLIAM,
ASSOCIATES. 273-2566
9250 Wilshire Blvd.,
Beverly Hills, Calif. (90212)

MESSENGER, FRED, AGENCY
654-3800
8265 Sunset Blvd. (90046)
M.E.W. COMPANY . . .   653-4731
151 N. San Vicente Blvd.,
Beverly Hills, Calif. (90211)
MILLER, STUART M., CO., THE
659-8131
8693 Wilshire Blvd., Suite 206
Beverly Hills, Calif. (90211)
MISHKIN AGENCY, INC., THE
274-5261
9255 Sunset Blvd. (90069)
MOLSON-STANTON ASSOCIATES
AGENCY, INC.   477-1262
10889 Wilshire Blvd., Suite 929
(90024)
MONTAIGNE, EVE, AGENCY
980-3779
10546 Burbank Blvd., Suite 3,
N. Hollywood, Calif. (91601)
MONTGOMERY, JO, AGENCY,
ARTISTS' MANAGER .   980-5899
4429 Carpenter Ave. (91604)
MOORE, LOLA, ARTIST MANAGER
276-6097
9172 Sunset Blvd. (90069)
MORRIS, WILLIAM, AGENCY, INC.
274-7451
151 El Camino, Beverly Hills,
Calif. (90212)   272-4111
1350 Avenue of the Americas,
New York, New York (10019)
(212) 586-5100
MOSS AGENCY, LTD. .   653-2900
113 N. San Vicente Blvd., Suite
302
Beverly Hills, Calif. (90211)
MOSS, MARVIN, ARTISTS'
MANAGER   274-8483

9200 Sunset Blvd., Suite 601
(90069)
MULTIMEDIA PRODUCT
DEVELOPMENT, INC..   276-6246
170 S. Beverly Dr., Beverly
Hills, Calif. (90212)
MURPHY, MARY, CONTESSA,
JOSEPH, AGENCY . . .   985-4241
10701 Riverside Dr., Toluca
Lake, Calif. (91602)
NOVEMBER NINTH MANAGEMENT
553-4123
9021 Melrose Ave., Suite 301
(90069)
OLIVER, MAURINE & ASSOCIATES
657-1250
8746 Sunset Blvd. (90069)
OTIS, DOROTHY DAY, AGENCY
461-4911
6430 Sunset Blvd., Suite 1203
(90028)
PEARSON, BEN, AGENCY
451-8414
606 Wilshire Blvd., Suite 614
(90401)
PICKMAN COMPANY, THE
273-8273
9025 Wilshire Blvd., Suite 303,
Beverly Hills, Calif. (90211)
PLESHETTE, LYNN, AGENCY
465-0428
2643 Creston Dr. (90068)
PORTNOY, MILDRED O., AGENCY
851-5426
11969 Ventura Blvd. (91604)
PREMIERE ARTISTS &
PRODUCTIONS AGENCY 651-3545
Artists' Manager
6399 Wilshire Blvd., Suite 506
(90048)

PROGRESSIVE ARTISTS AGENCY
553-8561
400 S. Beverly Dr., Beverly
Hills, Calif. (90212)
RAISON, ROBERT, ASSOCIATES
274-7217
9575 Lime Orchard Rd.,
Beverly Hills, Calif. (90210)
RAPER ENTERPRISES AGENCY
461-5033
6311 Yucca (90028)
ROBARDS, BILL, AGENCY 845-8547
4421 Riverside Dr., Toluca
Lake, Calif. (91505)
ROBINSON & ASSOCIATES, INC.
275-6114
132 S. Rodeo Dr., Beverly
Hills, Calif. (90212)
ROBINSON-WEINTRAUB &
ASSOCIATES, INC. . .   653-5802
554 S. San Vicente, Suite 3
(90048)
ROGERS, PHILIP & ASSOC.
275-5278
9046 Sunset Blvd. (90069)
ROSE, HAROLD, ARTISTS, LTD.
652-3961
8530 Wilshire Blvd., Beverly
Hills, Calif. (90211)
ROSEMARY MANAGEMENT
826-3453
11520 San Vicente Blvd., Suite
210 (90049)
RUBEN, SANDY ROTH   271-7209
9418 Wilshire Blvd., Beverly
Hills, Calif. (90212)
RUBY, BETTY, TALENT AGENCY
466-6652
1741 Ivar Ave., Suite 119
(90028)

SALKOW, IRVING, AGENCY
276-3141
450 N. Roxbury Dr., Beverly
Hills, Calif. (90210)
SCHALLERT, JOHN W. AGENCY
276-2044
450 N. Roxbury Dr., Beverly
Hills, Calif. (90210)
SCHECHTER, IRV, COMPANY
278-8070
404 N. Roxbury Dr., #800,
Beverly Hills, Calif. (90210)
SCHULLER, WILLIAM, AGENCY
273-4000
9110 Sunset Blvd. (90069)
SEALOCK, LOIS, AGENCY 473-7130
1609 Westwood Blvd.,
Suite 204 (90024)
SHAPIRA, DAVID & ASSOCIATES,
LTD..   278-2742
9171 Wilshire Blvd., Suite 525
Beverly Hills, Calif. (90210)
SHAPIRO-LICHTMAN, ARTISTS'
MANAGER   274-5235
9200 Sunset Blvd.
Penthouse Suite #7-8 (90069)
SHAW, GLENN, AGENCY
851-6262
3330 Barham Blvd., Suite 103
(90068)
SHEPHERD, DON, AGENCY
467-3535
1680 Vine Street, Suite 1105
(90028)
SHERMAN, CHARLIE, AGENCY
660-0000
6311 Yucca St. (90028)
SHERRELL, LEW, AGENCY, LTD.
461-9955
7060 Hollywood Blvd. (90028)

SIEGEL, JEROME, ASSOCIATES,
INC. 652-6033
8733 Sunset Blvd., Suite 202
(90069)

SINDELL AGENCY, THE   820-2069
11706 Montana Ave. (90049)

SOLOWAY, ARNOLD, ASSOCIATES
550-1300
118 S. Beverly Dr., Suite 226,
Beverly Hills, Calif. (90212)

STANLEY, MARGIE, AGENCY
466-3289
1418 N. Highland Ave. (90028)

STIEFEL OFFICE, THE .   274-7333
9255 Sunset Blvd., Suite 609
(90069)

STONER, PATRICIA, ARTISTS'
REPRESENTATIVES. .   980-4449
12069 Ventura Place (91604)

SUGHO, LARRY, AGENCY 657-1450
1017 N. La Cienega Blvd.,
Suite 303 (90069)

SWANSON, H.N., INC. .   652-5385
8523 Sunset Blvd. (90069)

TALENT, INC.   462-0913
1421 N. McCadden Place
(90028)

TANNEN, HERB & ASSOCIATES
466-6191
6640 Sunset Blvd., Suite 203
(90028)

TAYLOR, WILLIAM, AGENCY
550-7271
9000 Sunset Blvd., #805
(90069)

TOBIAS, HERB & ASSOCIATES, INC.
277-6211
1901 Avenue of the Stars, Suite
840 (90067)

TODD, DAVID &
CAMARILLO, JAMES. .   550-1790
9348 Santa Monica Blvd., Suite
101,
Beverly Hills, Calif. (90210)

TREJOS & TREJOS LITERARY
AGENCY, ARTISTS' MANAGER
538-2945
18235 Avalon Blvd., Carson,
Calif. (90746)

TRUE AGENCY.   874-8474
7513 Fountain (90046)

TWENTIETH CENTURY ARTISTS
990-8580
13273 Ventura Blvd., Suite 211
(91604)

UFLAND AGENCY, INC., THE
273-9441
190 N. Canon Dr., Beverly
Hills, Calif. (90210)

VITT, ANGIE, AGENCY   276-1646
9172 Sunset Blvd. (90069)

WEBB, RUTH   274-4311
9229 Sunset Blvd., Suite 509
(90069)

WEINER, JACK, AGENCY 652-1140
8721 Sunset Blvd. (90069)

WEINTRAUB, MURRY, AGENCY
274-6352
8230 Beverly Blvd., Suite 23
(90048)

WEITZMAN, LEW & ASSOCIATES
INC. 278-5562
9171 Wilshire Blvd., Suite 406
Beverly Hills, Calif. (90210)

WITZER, TED, AGENCY
278-1926
9441 Wilshire Blvd., Suite 214
Beverly Hills, Calif. (90212)

WORMSER, JACK, AGENCY, INC.
874-3050
1717 N. Highland Ave., Suite
414 (90028)
WOSK, SYLVIA, AGENCY 274-8063
439 S. La Cienega Blvd.
(90048)
DAN WRIGHT
c/o WRIGHT, ANN ASSOCIATES,
LTD.
8422 Melrose Place (90069)
655-5040
c/o WRIGHT, ANN
REPRESENTATIVES, INC.
136 East 57th Street,
New York, New York (10022)
(212) 832-0110

c/o WRIGHT, ANN
REPRESENTATIVES, INC.
333 Alcazar Ave.
Coral Gables, Fla.
(305) 445-2505
WRITERS & ARTISTS AGENCY
550-8030
9720 Wilshire Blvd., Beverly
Hills, Calif. (90212)
162 W. 56th St., New York,
New York (10019)
(212) 246-9029
ZIEGLER, DISKANT & ROTH, INC.
278-0070
9255 Sunset Blvd. (90069)

SCHOOLS AND PUBLICATIONS

In southern California two of the most highly respected theater arts programs in the country are offered at the University of California at Los Angeles (UCLA), Los Angeles 90024, and the University of Southern California (USC), University Park, Los Angeles 90007.

Others in southern California are the American Film Institute and the Sherwood Oaks Experimental College.

The American Film Institute is located at 501 Doheny Drive, Beverly Hills, Calif. 90210 (Phone: 213–278–8777). It offers two educational programs: (1) "A one-year structured Curriculum Program open to filmmakers who have obtained some proficiency in their craft. Individuals without experience in film who have experience in related fields—literature, theatre, music, photography and the fine arts—will also be considered." (2) "A Conservatory Program in which emphasis is placed on the work of the individual in his particular field of specialization. Members of this program are selected from among Fellows who have satisfactorily completed the

Curriculum Program." The annual tuition for the screenwriting program is $2,600. An endowed library is open to serious movie buffs and aspiring filmwriters. You may write for a catalog of their screenplay and television script collection.

The Sherwood Oaks Experimental College is located at 6353 Hollywood Boulevard, Hollywood, Calif. 90028 (Phone: 213–462–0669). Instruction in the various subjects is generally offered in six- to eight-week workshop courses. Tuition ranges from $40 to $350 per course. The average is $100 per course.

You will want to study as many screenplays as you can since there is no better way to learn the nuances of screenwriting. What you have learned in this book you can put to the test. Check the essential elements, see how they are developed. Study how narrative and dialog fully develop the plot, provide all necessary exposition, flow upward into crises, and sharply peak to the climax. Watch for the interplay between characters and the taut structure of the scenes. Time the length of the scenes. Whatever you do, don't try to imitate the style of a particular writer, no matter how highly you regard him.

PUBLISHERS

The publishers listed below publish books which contain film scripts. They will supply a list of these books upon request. You can order them through a bookstore.

Appleton-Century-Crofts, 292 Madison Avenue, New York, N.Y. 10017

Bantam Books, Inc., 666 Fifth Avenue, New York, N.Y. 10019

Grove Press, Inc., 53 E. 11th Street, New York, N.Y. 10003

Praeger Publications, 111 Fourth Avenue, New York, N.Y. 10003

Signet Books (New American Library), 1301 Avenue of the Americas, New York, N.Y. 10019

Simon and Schuster, Inc. (Modern Film Classics), 630 Fifth Avenue, New York, N.Y. 10020

Universe Books, Inc., 381 Park Avenue, New York, N.Y. 10016

Viking Press, Inc., 625 Madison Avenue, New York, N.Y. 10022

Yale University Press, 302 Temple Street, New Haven, Conn. 06511

Other universities and colleges which have exceptionally good theater arts programs include:

University of Chicago, Chicago, Ill. 60637
University of Texas, 200 E. 21st Street, Austin, Tex. 78712
Northwestern University, 619 Clark Street, Evanston, Ill. 60201
Columbia University, 630 W. 168th Street, New York, N.Y. 10032

Write to them for their catalogs if you are interested in studying filmwriting on this level. There are many universities and colleges which offer fine creative writing courses with special instruction in filmwriting. Contact those nearest you.

PUBLICATIONS

Ross Reports—lists all current TV shows and the names, addresses, and phone numbers of agents (Television Index Inc., 150 Fifth Avenue, New York, N.Y. 10011). For New York residents it is $1.55 per issue; for residents of other states, $1.45 per issue.

Television Market List—now published in the *Newsletter* of the Writers Guild of America, West—includes names of various series, and addresses and phone numbers of the producers and story editors of current shows. Send $2.00 to Blanche Baker at the Writers Guild address.

The Screenwriter's Handbook (Constance Nash and Virginia Oakey, Harper & Row, 1978) can be found in your local bookstore.

7

Excerpts from Teleplays and Treatments

The following excerpts from teleplays were selected to provide you with excellent examples of the specifics that have been discussed in the previous chapters. There is no better way to learn how to write teleplays than to study professional scripts—or portions of them which have been carefully researched to delineate every facet of teleplay writing.

The treatment excerpt is included to show you how its format is set up, what should be included within the first few pages (set and character descriptions, action, and some dialog), and the tempo it establishes for the ensuing narration.

EXCERPT FROM *THE ROOKIES* TELEPLAY *BLUE CHRISTMAS,* BY AARON SPELLING (REVISED FINAL DRAFT)

This scene includes excellent examples of characterization, exposition, and (as discussed in chapter 1) motivation. In the sensitively written character of Mrs. Lockett you are shown how her acute loneliness is amplified through her dialog, as are her gentleness, her maternal devotion, and her ultimate remorse over her action. The exposition is skillfully and subtly handled. You are so involved in the scene, you are unaware that all of the facts preceding her call to the police are being presented to you.

You are also shown (1) how the subject of the shot is written, (2) how narrative is written beneath it and inserted between two characters' dialog, (3) how there can be several camera angles (five) within a single scene, (4) how dialog is written, (5) how parenthetical directions are used, and (6) how you indicate that the script is continued from one page to the next. (Remember that the shots are numbered in this script because it is a shooting script; you will not use shot numbers in your script.)

On page 174, which is taken out of sequence, there are fine examples of a transitional instruction (DISSOLVE TO), STOCK SHOT (# 11), and PROCESS SHOT (# 12).

53F   INT. APT. no. 6 – NIGHT

It is overly decorated for Christmas . . . signs
of the Nativity everywhere. Terry and Chris,
guns drawn, look around.

                    TERRY
          Police . . . anybody home?

After a moment, the bedroom door (we do not see
bed room) opens timidly. MARGARET LOCKETT, a
little, bird-like lady in her sixties, enters
the living room.

                    CHRIS
          Police, ma'am. You reported
          a prowler.

                    MRS. LOCKETT
          That's right.

                    TERRY
          Your front door was unlocked . . .

                    MRS. LOCKETT
                (nods)
          So you could get in.

                    TERRY
          Would you get away from the door,
          ma'am.

She nods, steps aside. Terry, gun ready, moves
into the bedroom. CAMERA PANS and HOLDS on Chris
and Mrs. Lockett . . . beat later, Terry comes
out.

                    TERRY
                (continued)
          Clear there.
                              (CONTINUED)

                              MRS. LOCKETT
                         (motions)
                    He came up the fire escape . . .
                    over there.

                              CHRIS
                    I'll check it out.

Terry nods as Chris goes to window, opens it and
disappears.

                              TERRY
                    What happened, ma'am?

                              MRS. LOCKETT
                    Lockett . . . Mrs. Margaret Lockett.

                              TERRY
                    What happened, Mrs. Lockett?

                              MRS. LOCKETT
                    Well, I was making some ginger-
                    bread men . . .
                         (motions to tree)
                    . . . for my tree . . . when I heard a
                    noise. There was a man at my
                    window . . . standing on the fire
                    escape. I screamed . . . he ran . . .
                    and I called you.

                              TERRY
                    Could you give me a description
                    of him?

                              MRS. LOCKETT
                         (beat; thinks)
                    I . . . I really don't think so. It
                    all happened so fast.
                         (beat)
                    Officer, would you like something
                    . . . a sandwich, maybe?
                                        (CONTINUED)

                    TERRY
          No, thank you, ma'am.

                    MRS. LOCKETT
          A gingerbread man? I was just
          baking them!

                    TERRY
                (smiles)
          No, thank you.

                    MRS. LOCKETT
          You could take some with you . . .
          for tomorrow . . . do you have
          children?

                    TERRY
                (shakes his
                head)
          I'm not married.

                    MRS. LOCKETT
                (moving to
                kitchen)
          Oh, that's too bad. I'll get
          you some anyway. You know, I
          have a son about your age . . .
          he's not married, either.

                    TERRY
                (ill at ease)
          Yes, ma'am.

                    MRS. LOCKETT
          He was going to call me tonight . . .
          he's in New York . . . he calls me
                (MORE)

                              (CONTINUED)

                              MRS. LOCKETT (cont'd)
                    every holiday. He's a very good son.
                    Would you like some turkey?
                    I have lots of turkey.

                              TERRY
                    No, thank you. This man . . . you
                    did say it was a man, didn't you?

                              MRS. LOCKETT
                    Oh, yes . . . over six feet, I'd say.
                    You're sure you don't want to take
                    some turkey? My son loves turkey
                    . . . and dressing . . . I make very
                    good dressing, if I say so myself.

                              TERRY
                         (long look
                         at her)
                    How long has your son been in New
                    York, Mrs. Lockett?

                              MRS. LOCKETT
                    Four years . . . he's got a good job.
                    He's very good to me . . . he pays
                    for this apartment, you know.

                              TERRY
                    That's very nice.

                              MRS. LOCKETT
                         (suddenly)
                    What time is it?

                              TERRY
                         (surprised;
                         looks at
                         watch)
                    Eight minutes past ten.

                                        (CONTINUED)

                    MRS. LOCKETT
          I mean in New York.

                    TERRY
          That'd be eight past one in the
          morning.

                    MRS. LOCKETT
          He must be tied up . . . business.
          He always calls . . . every holiday.
          He never misses.

                    TERRY
          Well, it is very late . . . New York
          time.

                    MRS. LOCKETT
          Yes, that's it. I'm sure he must
          be tied up with business.

                    TERRY
             Probably.

53G ANOTHER ANGLE TOWARD WINDOW

     as Chris comes climbing through.

                    CHRIS
          Terry . . . can I see you?

     Puzzled, but not puzzled, Terry goes to him.

53H CLOSE SHOT TERRY AND CHRIS

     They speak in hushed voices.

                    TERRY
             What's up?

                              (CONTINUED)

                    CHRIS
          I went down the fire escape.

                    TERRY
          And?

                    CHRIS
          It's muddy down in the yard . . .
          they must have watered the place
          today.

                    TERRY
          So?

                    CHRIS
          There's no mud outside her window.
          How could anybody go through a
          muddy garden and not leave mud or
          footprints outside her window?

                    TERRY
               (beat)
          Okay, Chris.

                    CHRIS
          But, Terry, there's no way . . .

                    TERRY
               (fast)
          Okay, Chris.

He moves back to the lady, Chris following.

                    TERRY
               (continuing)
          I think it'll be all right now,
          ma'am.

                    MRS. LOCKETT
          You think it's safe?

                              (CONTINUED)

                    TERRY
          I'm sure it is.

She has a whole brown bag full.

                    MRS. LOCKETT
          I put some turkey in a bag . . .
          and some dressing. You can take
          It? I mean, it's not against
          the law to take a little tur-
          key, is it?

Chris looks to Terry, puzzled. Terry gives him a
quick look, then back to Mrs. Lockett.

                    TERRY
          No, ma'am . . . not at all.

He moves to her, takes the package.

                    MRS. LOCKETT
          You don't think he'll come back . . .
          whoever it was?

53I CLOSE SHOT-TERRY

looking deeply into her.

                    TERRY
          No, Mrs. Lockett . . . he won't come
          back.

53J CLOSE SHOT-MRS. LOCKETT   53J

looking at him . . . knowing that he knows.

                    MRS. LOCKETT
                 (long beat)
          Officer . . . I'm sorry . . . I . . .

Chris maybe a little mystified, but Terry knows the whole story.

> TERRY
> (quickly)
> Don't be sorry, Mrs. Lockett.
> That's why we're here. Call us
> whenever you need us.

> MRS. LOCKETT
> (quietly; only
> Terry will
> understand)
> I'm afraid I did.

> TERRY
> (softly)
> Goodnight, Mrs. Lockett . . .
> and Merry Christmas.

He touches Chris' arm, and the still puzzled Chris follows him to the door . . . and at that moment, the phone RINGS. INTERCHANGE CUTS between Terry and Mrs. Lockett - both of them hoping desperately. Then, she breaks and moves toward the phone. Terry and Chris watch.

> MRS. LOCKETT
> Hello . . . hello, Philip . . . no,
> no . . . it's not too late . . . Mer-
> ry Christmas to you . . . Sure, I
> knew you'd call . . . I never doubt-
> ed it for a moment . . .

EXCERPTS

11 INT. CAR - NIGHT (STOCK)

as our black-and-white cruises by.

12 INT. CAR - NIGHT (PROCESS)

> We see the lights of the street passing by. Both
> Terry and Chris are relaxed, just starting their
> shift.

> > CHRIS
> > Just doesn't feel like Christmas
> > that's all. I mean, how can you
> > get the Christmas spirit when
> > it's seventy degrees outside?

> > TERRY
> > (smiles)
> > I didn't know it was controlled
> > by a thermometer.

> > CHRIS
> > And this dumb city doesn't even
> > hang Xmas lights on the streets.

> > TERRY
> > This dumb city has an energy short-
> > age - or don't you read the papers?

> > CHRIS
> > And no snow. In Spokane, we've had
> > a white Christmas since I can remem-
> > ber. Sometimes two to three feet.

In shot number 11 the film editor will splice in a STOCK shot of
their black and white police car as it moves along the street.

In shot number 12 Chris and Terry would be sitting in a mock-up
patrol car in the studio on the set. In the background a street scene
would be flashing on a screen giving the impression that the car is
moving through traffic.

EXCERPT FROM *PHYLLIS* TELEPLAY
YOU'RE NOT GETTING BETTER, JUST OLDER,
BY DAVID LLOYD (FINAL DRAFT)

This is a fine example of how the 30-minute situation comedy is set up on the page (in contrast to the screenplay format used in *The Rookies*). The dialog is double-spaced, centered on the page. Narrative is in caps and single-spaced. There is, too, you will notice, a difference in the way parenthetical directions are handled. The left margins are about 1¾ inches wide; the right margins are about 2½ inches wide.

This final portion of a scene is a good example of how action rises to the climax (when Mary capitulates and decides she cannot end her friendship with Phyllis, after all). Following the climax and the end of Act II, there is the 1½-page Tag which ties the final knot on the plot and ends the teleplay.

MARY

Okay, I accept that. I . . .

forgive you. It's done, it's

over. Let's just drop it.

(SHE OPENS FRONT DOOR) So

long, Phyllis.

PHYLLIS SADLY PUTS PAPER HAT ON HER
HEAD AND, SITTING SLUMPED FORWARD,
STARING AT THE CANDLE ON HER CAKE,
BEGINS TO SING MOURNFULLY
TO HERSELF:

PHYLLIS (CONT'D)

(SINGING) Happy birthday to me . . .

                    MARY

          Aw, Phyllis, don't do this -

                   PHYLLIS

          (SAME) Happy birthday to me . . .

                    MARY

          - Because I've got to leave,

          and that's that. I'm sorry.

MARY TAKES A STEP OUT THE FRONT DOOR.

                   PHYLLIS

          (SAME) Happy birthday, dear

          Phyllis . . .

MARY COMES BACK IN THE DOOR AND CROSSES TO
HER. IT'S ALL OVER.

                    MARY

          (TEARY) Aw, Phyllis . . . !

SHE SITS ON THE COUCH. THEY HUG. PHYLLIS
TAKES ANOTHER PAPER HAT OUT OF THE BAG AND
PUTS IT ON MARY'S HEAD. TOGETHER THEY SING
LAST LINE.

                    BOTH

          (SINGING) Happy birthday to

          you/me.

PHYLLIS BLOWS OUT THE CANDLE AND SMILES AT
MARY, WHO SMILES BACK AS WE:

                                   FADE OUT:

               END OF ACT TWO

<u>TAG</u>

FADE IN:

JONATHAN'S LIVING ROOM A HALF HOUR LATER
MARY AND PHYLLIS ARE FINISHING THEIR CAKE.

MARY

That was delicious.

PHYLLIS

Thank you so much for staying, Mary.

I feel terrible about having made

you miss your plane.

MARY

That's alright. Planes come and

go. But friendships like ours

you just can't get rid of.

THE DOOR OPENS AND <u>MOTHER DEXTER ENTERS.</u>

PHYLLIS

Good evening, Mother Dexter.

MOTHER DEXTER

Ah, the birthday girl! And I see

all your friends have arrived.

PHYLLIS

Oh, you two saw each other last
night, but I didn't get a chance
to introduce you properly. Mother
Dexter, this is my very dear friend,
Mary Richards.

MARY

It's so nice to meet you, Mother
Dexter. Phyllis has told me
all about you.

MOTHER DEXTER

She's told me all about you, too.
(SWEETLY) Tell me, are you still
a virgin?

MARY

(JUST AS SWEETLY) Were you ever one?

MOTHER DEXTER

(TO PHYLLIS) I like your friend.

AS MOTHER DEXTER EXITS WE,

FADE OUT.

THE END

EXCERPT FROM A TREATMENT FOR THE TELEPLAY *KINGDOM IN THE DUST,* BY ISABELLE ZIEGLER

In these excellent opening pages of a treatment you will see how the first page is set up, how the setting is described, how all principal characters are introduced (in caps as they first appear), and how the central conflict is revealed. This is not a complete act but within it there are seven important scene changes. It contains very brief character descriptions, yet, through exposition in both dialog and visuals, the characters of the protagonist and antagonist (Don and Hardy, respectively) are clearly revealed. You will notice that dialog is confined to exposition and character revelation; there is no irrelevant dialog. This entire treatment is 35 pages long—for a 120-minute movie for television.

EXCERPTS FROM AN OUTLINE FOR THE TELEVISION SERIES *STELLA FORTUNE,* BY CONSTANCE NASH

In these two pages of outline you will see how theme is handled, how the principal characters are introduced, and how the series will continue to play off the plot-within-a-plot. You will notice that dialog is not included in a concise outline. Nor is a story revealed. The entire presentation consists of two pages of outline, 22 pages of script excerpt, and three pages of 12 episodic synopses.

"KINGDOM IN THE DUST"
Written by
Isabelle Ziegler
11/23/76

SETTING

Gorham, a small South Texas county seat in the 1970s—population: 10,000 Anglos, 15,000 Mexican-Americans. The town had earlier gone almost overnight from cattle town to oil town, from horse to Cadillac. There are swimming pools without water and lawns without grass because heavy gritty dust, carried across the desert by winds from the Gulf of Mexico, sweeps constantly over the town. There are no sidewalks because nobody in Gorham walks except children and Mexican-Americans.

ACT ONE

A colorful fiesta is in progress at the Hardy Wright ranch, with hundreds of persons gathered to celebrate the election of young DON LAUGHTON as county attorney. There are mariachi bands strolling through the crowd, costumed Spanish dancers, several pits in which whole steers are being barbecued, long plank tables loaded with food and drink. In the center of all this activity rises a platform festooned with the Lone Star flags of Texas.

We see on the platform Don Laughton, who is hatless and wears slacks and loafers in a community where all males affect Stetsons, levis, and high-heeled cowboy boots. He holds both hands aloft, smiling and waving at the crowd, many of whom carry large signs: *Don Laughton for County Attorney* and similar slogans.

On the platform with him are four other persons. In ensuing scenes we learn that they are: PENNY, his wife, and BILLY, his son, who share an aura of great warmth and joy; HARDY WRIGHT, who is the host and the autocratic leader of the county; and FIDEL CORTINO, Don's campaign manager, who has the patrician Castilian features of his Spanish forebears. The adults are in their middle 30's; Billy is eight years old.

After the crowd becomes quiet, Don makes a brief "Thank-you-and-let's-get-on-with-the-party" speech, then drops from the platform to circulate through the crowd. A woman, obviously drunk, screams at him that he has damn little to celebrate since he didn't really win the election; it was bought for him by Hardy Wright. Fidel, who is walking with him, shrugs and says, "She's only the first. You'll get used to it."

Don, troubled and curious, urges Hardy Wright to go with him to the ranch house where they can talk in private. In his office, Hardy admits that he not only has been paying the Mexicans' poll taxes but when necessary has also paid them to vote. (Mexican-Americans will be referred to from here on only as Mexicans.) Don is enraged. He says that he has been too long away from Gorham, practicing law in Austin, and too busy campaigning day and night to know what was going on. He intends to resign immediately.

"Grow up, Don," Hardy says, "I just greased the wheels a little. It's a fact of political life."

"Of course, but not *my* political life," Don says.

"You needed the votes and you got 'em. Now why in hell don't you use 'em to keep all those high-minded campaign promises you made?"

Despite his initial anger, Don allows Hardy to convince him that he can best serve the Mexicans and the poor Anglos of the county by remaining in office.

Driving home from the fiesta, Don tells Penny the facts about how he won the election and bitterly attacks his old friend and campaign manager, Fidel, for not warning him.

"You know that he's Hardy's man," Penny says, "bought and paid for a long time ago."

From the ensuing dialog we learn that Hardy holds the mortgages on Fidel's bankrupt ancestral ranch and elegant manor house. Fidel's adored sister, MAGDA, is Hardy's mistress and for her sake, against the day Hardy will surely get tired of her, Fidel is determined to keep his ranch at any price. That price is his servitude to Hardy, to whom he is invaluable because he is the acknowledged, almost revered, spokesman for all the Mexicans.

OUTLINE
"STELLA FORTUNE"
BY
Constance Nash
7/25/77

A series concept based upon the bigger-than-life figure of STELLA FORTUNE. In reality Stella is a plain, uninspiring young woman who works as a librarian in a branch of the New York Public Library.

Stella's heroic deeds all take place in her fantasy life; she makes the transition from a hair-netted, sexless looking mouse through Fade-outs which propel her into her fantastic secret life.

In her fantasy life she is ineffably lovely, curvy, self-confident, composed, and brilliant. Nothing is too difficult for her to deal with or solve. And she cannot help being a femme fatale—men fall at her feet—which she takes in stride.

Stella's fantasies come about through books. In her role as librarian, books are the vehicles to specific fantasies. Such as: Black Gold Diplomacy wherein Stella is Ms. Fortune, diplomat, negotiating for oil with OPEC Sheik who finds her asexual. Until her transformation as a belly dancer and the mysterious woman in his life. She gets contract for America. Or World War II Heroics (see attached script excerpt) wherein Stella is Lt. Fortune, pilot, shot down over Pacific Japanese-held island. She has to rescue General Hadsen, who is a caged POW. Her feat is daring.

The continuing plot revolves around SCOTT HADSEN. His role is as versatile as Stella's because he appears as her super romantic interest in every fantasy; if not romantic he is definitely a worthy antagonist who (very) occasionally gets the upper hand.

Scott is quite dapper, a man about town, urbane and polished; all the qualities Stella longs for in a man and finds in novels. Her whole life is spent in books. Until now.

Scott is an agent for GASP, a division of a CIA-like organization. GASP is an acronym meaning Get Agents Soon Please. Their primary function is to keep a 24-hour surveillance on foreign spies. In addition, their current assignment is to thwart the exchange of top-secret military microfilm, being implanted in books, among the agents and double agents for the USSR, China, and Cuba.

GASP has discovered that espionage agents are meeting in the branch of the library. But their activities are intercepted and thwarted by Stella's inadvertent tidying.

GASP decides to induct Stella into their organization without actually informing her about it.

Stella has an overwhelming infatuation for Scott, which makes her more bumbling than she normally would be around him. Of course, he never notices her as a romantic interest.

At her rooming house, run by BIRD, a well-meaning woman in her fifties who stuffs herself into too-small dresses and flirts with everything male, are Stella's two friends, CECIL and ROGER FARCKLE, brothers. They are a would-be musical comedy team, yet to be hired. To make a living, they run a seedy detective agency that specializes in bigamy and related problems—missing persons and amnesiacs.

Cecil bumbles into the intrigue running rampant around Stella in the library, but doesn't notice. It takes Roger to figure something is afoot. Things get worse before they're better.

We see STELLA FORTUNE as a one-camera show with permanent sets such as the library, the rooming house, GASP headquarters, Scott's swank apartment, and the detective agency complete with a stage.

Index